The Cloud Puzzle Solved: Azure Design Patterns

Kameron Hussain and Frahaan Hussain

Published by Sonar Publishing, 2025.

THE CLOUD PUZZLE SOLVED: AZURE DESIGN PATTERNS

First edition. April 26, 2025.

ISBN: 979-8231239580

Written by Kameron Hussain and Frahaan Hussain.

The Cloud Puzzle Solved: Azure Design Patterns

First Edition

Preface

The cloud revolution has transformed how businesses build and scale applications, and Microsoft Azure sits at the heart of this transformation. As more organizations migrate to the cloud or adopt hybrid strategies, understanding core architectural principles and proven design patterns becomes not only valuable but necessary for building resilient, scalable, and secure solutions.

This book, "**The Cloud Puzzle Solved: Azure Design Patterns**", is designed for architects, developers, and IT professionals who are beginning their Azure journey or looking to solidify their understanding of cloud-native design. By blending practical insights with real-world examples, this guide equips you with the knowledge to design efficient, scalable, and secure cloud solutions using Azure.

Starting with the fundamentals of cloud architecture and the core principles that underpin all successful cloud solutions, the book progresses to explore key Azure services, architectural design patterns, high-performance strategies, and advanced topics such as serverless computing and event-driven design. Each chapter is structured to build upon the last, offering a logical progression from introductory concepts to complex architectures.

You will find dedicated chapters on security, resiliency, data-driven design, and real-world case studies that bring all these concepts together in practical applications. Whether you're building a new system from scratch, modernizing an existing monolith, or designing a data-intensive application, the patterns and practices explored in this book will serve as essential tools in your Azure toolkit.

I invite you to approach this book not just as a guide, but as a foundation for innovation. Embrace the principles, explore the patterns, and most importantly, start building.

Let's dive into the cloud—Azure style.

Table of Contents

G

H

I

J

K

L

M

N

O

P

Q

R

S

T

U

V

W

Summary

Resources for Further Learning

Official Microsoft Azure Documentation

Chapter 1: Introduction to Azure and Cloud Design Patterns

The Evolution of Cloud Architecture

In the early days of computing, organizations relied heavily on monolithic, on-premises infrastructure to support their applications and services. These environments required significant upfront investment in hardware, skilled personnel to maintain the infrastructure, and had limited flexibility to scale based on user demand. Any changes in load—expected or not—could cause system outages or degraded performance, leading to poor user experiences and financial loss.

As user expectations grew and systems became increasingly complex, businesses started seeking alternatives that offered greater agility, scalability, and cost-efficiency. This led to the rise of virtualization and eventually cloud computing.

The First Wave: Virtualization

Virtualization marked a pivotal shift. By decoupling applications from physical hardware, businesses could run multiple applications on a single physical server through virtual machines (VMs). This not only improved hardware utilization but also introduced the concept of scalability without increasing physical infrastructure.

Yet, virtualization was only a stepping stone.

The Cloud Era: IaaS, PaaS, and SaaS

Cloud computing formalized resource sharing at scale. It introduced three primary service models:

- **Infrastructure as a Service (IaaS):** Offers virtualized computing resources over the internet. Example: Azure Virtual Machines.

- **Platform as a Service (PaaS):** Provides hardware and software tools over the internet, typically for application development. Example: Azure App Service.

- **Software as a Service (SaaS):** Delivers software applications over the web on a subscription basis. Example: Microsoft 365.

Azure, launched by Microsoft in 2010, quickly became one of the leading cloud platforms, enabling organizations to deploy global-scale applications with unprecedented ease and flexibility.

The Rise of Cloud-Native Architecture

As cloud adoption matured, the emphasis shifted toward designing applications that truly leverage the cloud's capabilities. These "cloud-native" applications are architected to maximize scalability, resilience, and agility. They typically exhibit characteristics such as:

- **Microservices architecture**

- **API-first design**

- **Event-driven interactions**

- **Infrastructure as code (IaC)**

- **Automated CI/CD pipelines**

Azure provides comprehensive support for these patterns through services like Azure Kubernetes Service (AKS), Azure Functions, Logic Apps, Azure DevOps, and Azure API Management.

Key Milestones in Cloud Evolution

Year	Milestone
2006	AWS launches EC2 (start of modern cloud era)
2010	Microsoft Azure launched
2015	Azure introduces App Services, Functions (serverless)
2017	Kubernetes gains traction; AKS later introduced
2020	Hybrid and multi-cloud strategies rise
2023	Cloud AI services like Azure OpenAI gain adoption

The cloud has evolved from a flexible hosting environment to a strategic enabler of innovation, agility, and resilience. Today, the focus is no longer just on migrating to the cloud, but on architecting for the cloud.

Azure's Role in Modern Architecture

Azure's global presence, breadth of services, and enterprise integration make it a preferred platform for organizations ranging from startups to large enterprises. Key attributes include:

- **Global availability:** Data centers in more than 60 regions.
- **Security and compliance:** Comprehensive certifications including ISO, HIPAA, and GDPR.
- **Integrated development tools:** Native support for Visual Studio, GitHub Actions, and Azure DevOps.

- **Advanced analytics and AI:** Tools like Synapse, Azure ML, and OpenAI APIs.

These capabilities empower architects to build intelligent applications that not only scale efficiently but also adapt in real time to changing business needs.

Shift from Monolith to Modular Architectures

Traditional monolithic applications bundled all functionalities into a single deployable unit. This posed challenges in terms of deployment agility, scalability, and team ownership.

Cloud-native applications, in contrast, are often composed of microservices. Each service is independently deployable, responsible for a specific business capability, and communicates over APIs. Azure supports this architecture through:

- **Azure Kubernetes Service (AKS):** Container orchestration.

- **Azure Container Apps:** Serverless containers for microservices.

- **Azure API Management:** For secure and scalable API exposure.

�# Example: Simple Bicep snippet for deploying an Azure Container App

resource containerApp 'Microsoft.App/containerApps@2022-03-01' = {

name: 'my-container-app'

```
location: resourceGroup().location

properties: {

managedEnvironmentId:
'/subscriptions/.../managedEnvironments/myEnv'

configuration: {

ingress: {

external: true

targetPort: 80

}

}

template: {

containers: [

{

name: 'my-app'

image: 'myregistry.azurecr.io/myapp:v1'

}

]

}

}

}
```

�This declarative infrastructure-as-code snippet defines an Azure Container App and demonstrates the shift toward treating infrastructure as programmable, repeatable, and scalable.

The Importance of Cloud Patterns

As cloud environments grow in complexity, best practices become essential to avoid pitfalls such as vendor lock-in, unscalable solutions, or insecure configurations. This is where **cloud design patterns** play a critical role.

Design patterns are time-tested solutions to common architectural problems. In the context of Azure, these might include:

- Implementing **asynchronous messaging** with Azure Service Bus
- Using **API Gateway** pattern with Azure API Management
- Applying **Circuit Breaker** to ensure resilience
- Leveraging **CQRS and Event Sourcing** for data integrity

Each pattern encapsulates a proven approach, ensuring that your architecture remains robust under changing conditions and evolving requirements.

Looking Ahead

This book delves deep into these architectural patterns, but always from a practical, real-world standpoint. You'll explore how to:

- Identify the right pattern for a specific use case

- Understand trade-offs in applying the pattern
- Implement the pattern using Azure-native services

The goal is to not only give you a reference but to empower you with **architectural thinking**—so you can confidently design cloud solutions that are scalable, secure, resilient, and cost-effective.

By the end of this book, you'll be equipped with the tools and mindset needed to architect the next generation of applications in the Microsoft Azure ecosystem.

Why Design Patterns Matter in Azure

As enterprises increasingly adopt cloud-native architectures, they often encounter complex design challenges involving scalability, availability, cost, integration, and security. To navigate this intricate landscape, architects and developers turn to design patterns—proven solutions to recurring problems that help standardize and streamline cloud architecture. These patterns are particularly significant in Azure, a platform that offers an expansive ecosystem of tools and services.

Design patterns are more than just blueprints; they are strategic instruments that guide architectural decisions, reduce technical debt, and ensure long-term maintainability of cloud systems. In the context of Azure, they enable efficient use of native services while aligning with best practices and compliance standards.

The Role of Design Patterns in Cloud-Native Architecture

Cloud-native development embraces principles such as microservices, API-first development, continuous delivery, and dynamic scaling. However, without a structured approach to architecture, teams may inadvertently introduce inefficiencies and risks.

Design patterns provide:

- **Consistency:** Ensures uniformity across services and components, simplifying development, maintenance, and onboarding.
- **Resilience:** Encourages defensive coding through fallback strategies like retries and circuit breakers.
- **Performance Optimization:** Supports caching, asynchronous processing, and distributed computing.
- **Security Assurance:** Standardizes approaches to authentication, authorization, and data protection.
- **Cost Management:** Enables efficient resource usage through patterns like serverless and auto-scaling.

In Azure, patterns serve as architectural guardrails. They allow you to build systems that are not only technically sound but also operationally mature and aligned with Azure's capabilities.

Categorization of Azure Design Patterns

To better understand how patterns apply to Azure, it's helpful to group them into categories based on their focus:

Category	Example Patterns	Primary Azure Services
Scalability	Auto-scaling, Queue-Based Load Leveling	Azure Functions, Azure Service Bus, Azure Scale Sets
Resiliency	Retry, Circuit Breaker, Bulkhead	Azure Application Gateway, Azure API Management
Security	Gateway Offloading, Identity Propagation	Azure AD, Key Vault, Azure Front Door
Data	Event Sourcing, CQRS, Data Sharding	Cosmos DB, Synapse, Event Hubs
Performance	Caching, Throttling, Content Delivery	Azure Redis Cache, Azure CDN
Monitoring	Health Endpoint, Log Aggregation	Azure Monitor, Application Insights

By adopting patterns from each category, developers can address a wide range of design goals, from handling transient failures to building real-time data pipelines.

Common Challenges Without Design Patterns

Let's consider a few scenarios that highlight the pitfalls of ignoring design patterns:

- **Monolithic Bottlenecks:** A tightly coupled architecture causes the entire application to redeploy even for minor changes, increasing downtime.

- **Over-provisioning Resources:** Without auto-scaling, apps run on over-provisioned VMs to handle peak traffic, leading to unnecessary costs.

- **Single Point of Failure:** Lack of redundancy and health checks causes outages during component failures.

- **Security Gaps:** Missing centralized authentication or improper secrets management exposes the application to breaches.

Azure provides mechanisms to solve each of these, but knowing how and when to apply them requires architectural clarity—a benefit delivered by design patterns.

Real-World Use Case: E-Commerce Checkout System

Imagine an e-commerce platform built on Azure. The checkout process involves multiple steps: payment processing, inventory update, shipping coordination, and customer notification. Implementing this as a synchronous pipeline leads to poor user experience and potential data loss.

Without patterns:

- Delays in shipping system affect payment confirmation.
- Any failure leads to rollback of the entire transaction.
- System becomes fragile and hard to scale.

With patterns:

- **Queue-Based Load Leveling** allows the checkout request to be placed into a queue.
- **Event-Driven Design** decouples inventory, payment, and notification processes.
- **Retry Pattern** ensures transient failures are retried without user impact.

- **Compensation Transactions** handle business logic rollback if needed.

Azure Services Used:

- Azure Service Bus for queuing
- Azure Functions for processing events
- Azure Event Grid for coordination
- Azure Cosmos DB for order data
- Azure Monitor for observability

```
// Sample Azure Function (Node.js) for processing queue messages
module.exports = async function (context, myQueueItem) {
context.log('Processing order: ', myQueueItem.orderId);
try {
await processPayment(myQueueItem.paymentDetails);
await updateInventory(myQueueItem.items);
await sendConfirmationEmail(myQueueItem.email);
context.log('Order processed successfully');
} catch (err) {
context.log.error('Error processing order:', err.message);
throw err; // Will retry depending on host.json settings
}
```

```
};
```

By applying these patterns, the e-commerce platform becomes resilient, scalable, and user-friendly.

Azure Design Pattern Lifecycle

Patterns in Azure aren't static templates. They evolve as the platform evolves. Adopting a pattern involves several stages:

1. **Identification:** Define the architectural problem (e.g., how to handle burst traffic).
2. **Pattern Selection:** Choose the most suitable pattern (e.g., Queue-Based Load Leveling).
3. **Service Mapping:** Identify Azure services that implement or support this pattern.
4. **Implementation:** Configure and deploy using ARM/Bicep/Terraform or the Azure Portal.
5. **Monitoring and Optimization:** Continuously assess system performance and iterate.

This lifecycle is iterative. Patterns often evolve alongside product releases, requiring regular architectural reviews.

Design Patterns vs Anti-Patterns

Design patterns are positive solutions, but there are also **anti-patterns**—common mistakes or poor practices that lead to suboptimal outcomes. Recognizing these is equally critical.

Anti-Pattern	Description	Better Pattern
Big Ball of Mud	Lack of modularity, hard to scale	Microservices
Synchronous Everything	Tight coupling, poor performance	Event-Driven Architecture
Hardcoded Configs	Difficult to change or secure	External Configuration with Azure App Configuration
Direct Database Access from UI	Security and logic issues	API Gateway with proper abstraction
Monitored by Console Logs Only	Limited visibility	Centralized Logging and Alerts via Application Insights

Avoiding these anti-patterns and replacing them with proven strategies elevates both the robustness and maintainability of your solution.

When to Apply Patterns in the Software Lifecycle

Design patterns should not be treated as one-size-fits-all solutions. Timing and context are everything.

- **During Initial Design:** Start with patterns like Microservices, API Gateway, and Identity Federation.

- **During Scaling:** Introduce Auto-Scaling, Caching, and Throttling.

- **During Hardening:** Apply Security, Retry, and Circuit Breaker patterns.

- **During Optimization:** Use patterns for Cost Management and Observability.

Azure provides architectural frameworks like the **Microsoft Cloud Adoption Framework (CAF)** and **Well-Architected Framework** to guide this journey, with embedded references to patterns at each stage.

The Azure Well-Architected Framework

Microsoft's Well-Architected Framework breaks cloud architecture into five pillars:

1. **Cost Optimization**
2. **Operational Excellence**
3. **Performance Efficiency**
4. **Reliability**
5. **Security**

Each pillar aligns with a suite of design patterns. For instance:

- **Reliability:** Circuit Breaker, Retry, Load Leveling

- **Security:** Role-Based Access Control, Token Authentication

- **Performance:** CDN, Cache-Aside Pattern

Understanding how patterns reinforce these pillars helps architects design not just for function but for excellence.

Conclusion

In the Azure ecosystem, design patterns are foundational elements that bring structure, repeatability, and best practices to your cloud solutions. They enable you to:

- Architect with foresight rather than hindsight.
- Minimize risk and technical debt.
- Optimize for scale, cost, and resilience.

Patterns do not replace creativity or innovation; they **channel** them. They empower you to build with confidence, knowing that your design choices are backed by real-world validation and supported by Azure's robust service offerings.

As you progress through this book, each subsequent chapter will explore specific patterns in depth—what problems they solve, how to implement them using Azure, and how to measure their effectiveness. Understanding **why** these patterns matter is the first step in mastering the art and science of Azure cloud architecture.

Goals of This Book

This book aims to serve as a comprehensive guide for beginners and intermediate professionals navigating the vast and sometimes overwhelming world of cloud architecture in Microsoft Azure. Its primary objective is to demystify cloud-native design and architecture by grounding the reader in practical patterns, services, and methodologies that apply to real-world scenarios.

Azure is a powerful platform, but power alone isn't enough. Architects, developers, and DevOps engineers must understand how to use that power effectively and responsibly. This book is designed to give you that understanding. It goes beyond tutorials and reference documentation, offering contextual knowledge about *why* you would use a particular service or pattern—not just *how*.

The Purpose Behind the Pages

The cloud is not just an infrastructure shift—it's a paradigm shift. Organizations moving to the cloud often realize that simply lifting and shifting existing applications results in limited benefits. To fully harness the cloud's potential, applications must be architected for scale, resiliency, performance, and security. That's where cloud-native design and architectural patterns come into play.

This book is meant to:

- Equip you with foundational knowledge of Azure's core services
- Teach you how to apply architectural design patterns effectively
- Show you how to solve real-world challenges using Azure-native tools
- Help you design systems that are scalable, resilient, secure, and cost-effective
- Give you the architectural vocabulary to contribute meaningfully to design discussions
- Prepare you to confidently undertake cloud projects and migrations

By the end of this book, you will be able to design Azure-based solutions that go far beyond simple deployments. You'll be able to identify trade-offs, optimize for performance, secure your systems, and monitor them in production.

Who This Book is For

This book is primarily written for:

- **Software Developers and Engineers:** Who want to build scalable and maintainable cloud-native applications on Azure.

- **Solutions Architects:** Who are tasked with designing cloud-based systems with high performance, availability, and security.

- **DevOps Engineers and SREs:** Who need to understand the underlying architectural decisions to build CI/CD pipelines, automate deployments, and ensure observability.

- **IT Professionals and SysAdmins:** Looking to upskill and adapt to cloud-native infrastructure and services.

- **Students and Self-Learners:** Who want to establish a solid foundation in Azure architecture.

No prior experience with Azure is assumed, though familiarity with cloud computing concepts and software development will be helpful.

A Pattern-Centric Approach

Rather than focusing solely on services or tools, this book takes a **pattern-centric approach**. Each chapter introduces design patterns that address specific challenges in cloud architecture. Once introduced, these patterns are mapped to Azure services and brought to life through detailed examples and case studies.

For example:

- The **Retry Pattern** is discussed in the context of transient failures and implemented using **Azure Functions**, **Service Bus**, and **Polly** for retries.
- The **CQRS Pattern** is introduced for complex read/write segregation, demonstrated with **Cosmos DB**, **Event Hubs**, and **Azure Functions**.
- The **API Gateway Pattern** is explained with **Azure API Management**, complete with policies for throttling, transformation, and security.

Each pattern discussion includes:

- The architectural problem it solves
- Benefits and trade-offs
- Implementation details using Azure services
- Real-world application scenarios
- Common pitfalls and anti-patterns to avoid

This structure ensures that your understanding is both conceptual and practical—ideal for both exam preparation and job execution.

Azure-Native Focus

There are many cloud providers, but this book is explicitly focused on **Microsoft Azure**. Azure's breadth and depth—from its foundational IaaS offerings to high-level AI and analytics services—make it an ideal platform to learn cloud architecture comprehensively.

The book will guide you through the practical use of services such as:

- **Compute:** Virtual Machines, App Services, Kubernetes Service (AKS), Azure Functions
- **Storage:** Blob Storage, Files, Tables, Queues
- **Databases:** Azure SQL, Cosmos DB, PostgreSQL
- **Networking:** VNets, Azure Front Door, Load Balancer, Application Gateway
- **Security:** Azure Active Directory, Key Vault, Azure Firewall
- **DevOps:** Azure DevOps, GitHub Actions, ARM Templates, Bicep
- **Monitoring and Observability:** Azure Monitor, Application Insights, Log Analytics
- **Integration:** Logic Apps, Event Grid, Service Bus, API Management

Each of these services will be presented not in isolation, but in context—how they work together to support the patterns and strategies discussed.

Emphasis on Real-World Scenarios

Theory is essential, but cloud architecture is a discipline rooted in real-world constraints. Throughout the book, you'll encounter **case studies**, **scenarios**, and **sample architectures** that reflect real enterprise needs.

For example:

- A **FinTech** case study using **Event Sourcing and Secure DevOps**
- An **eCommerce platform** scaling globally with **API Gateway and CDN patterns**
- A **data analytics pipeline** combining **Data Lake**, **Synapse**, and **Stream Analytics**
- A **legacy monolith migration** to **microservices** using the **Strangler Fig Pattern**

Each case study explores architectural decisions, implementation steps, and the rationale behind each choice—giving you insight into how theory translates into actual deployments.

Code-First, But Not Code-Only

Azure is a highly programmable platform, and this book reflects that. Expect to see:

- **Infrastructure as Code (IaC):** Using Bicep, ARM templates, or Terraform
- **Function Code Examples:** In C#, JavaScript, or Python

- **Pipeline Definitions:** For CI/CD automation
- **Monitoring Queries:** Using KQL (Kusto Query Language)

Here's a sample Bicep module for deploying a resilient web app infrastructure:

```
module appService 'modules/appService.bicep' = {
name: 'webApp'
params: {
location: resourceGroup().location
name: 'myWebApp'
sku: 'S1'
}
}
module sqlDb 'modules/sqlDatabase.bicep' = {
name: 'appDb'
params: {
location: resourceGroup().location
dbName: 'appDb'
}
}
```

This encourages an infrastructure-as-code mindset from the start, ensuring reproducibility, scalability, and traceability.

Preparing You for What's Next

The technology landscape is always evolving. Today's best practices may change tomorrow. However, the **patterns**, **principles**, and **mental models** you'll learn in this book are evergreen. Once you understand the **why**, you can easily adapt to changes in **how** services are delivered or structured.

You'll also find resources for ongoing learning, including:

- Microsoft Learn modules
- GitHub repositories for reference architectures
- Links to Azure documentation
- Suggestions for certifications (like AZ-305 and AZ-700)

The aim is not only to teach you Azure today but to prepare you for continuous growth in your career as a cloud architect or engineer.

Summary of Book Objectives

To summarize, this book will help you:

1. Understand the core principles of cloud-native architecture
2. Learn and apply proven architectural design patterns
3. Build secure, scalable, and cost-effective systems using Azure services
4. Navigate real-world use cases and scenarios
5. Use infrastructure-as-code and automation for production-

ready deployments
6. Monitor, maintain, and evolve cloud applications post-deployment
7. Develop critical thinking and pattern recognition for architecture decisions

Armed with this knowledge, you'll be able to approach Azure with confidence—whether you're designing greenfield applications, modernizing legacy systems, or managing hybrid environments.

Let's now step into the architectural foundations that underpin all great Azure solutions.

Chapter 2: Core Principles of Cloud Architecture

Scalability and Elasticity

Scalability and elasticity are foundational principles in cloud architecture, enabling applications to dynamically adapt to changing workloads without requiring manual intervention or causing service degradation. While they are often used interchangeably, these concepts have distinct meanings and implications for solution design in Microsoft Azure.

Scalability refers to a system's ability to handle increased load by adding resources—either vertically (scaling up) or horizontally (scaling out).

Elasticity extends this concept by introducing automation and responsiveness, allowing the system to scale resources in or out automatically, in real-time, based on demand.

Both principles are vital for ensuring performance, cost-efficiency, and user satisfaction.

Types of Scalability

Azure supports multiple scaling approaches, which can be leveraged based on the type of service and workload characteristics.

Vertical Scaling (Scale Up)

This involves increasing the power (CPU, memory, IOPS) of existing instances. It's simple to implement but has limits and may result in downtime during upgrades.

Example:

Increasing the pricing tier of an Azure App Service from B1 to P1V3 to gain more compute resources.

```
{
"sku": {
"name": "P1V3",
"tier": "PremiumV3",
"capacity": 1
}
}
```

Horizontal Scaling (Scale Out)

This involves increasing the number of instances of a service. It offers better fault tolerance and is often combined with load balancing.

Example:

Scaling out an Azure Kubernetes Service (AKS) node pool to handle additional microservices.

```
az aks nodepool scale \
—resource-group myResourceGroup \
—cluster-name myAKSCluster \
—name nodepool1 \
—node-count 5
```

Elasticity: Automated Scaling

Elasticity allows systems to scale automatically based on real-time demand, optimizing resource usage and cost. Azure services like **App Service**, **Virtual Machine Scale Sets**, **Azure Functions**, and **AKS** offer auto-scaling capabilities.

Azure App Service Auto-Scaling

Azure App Service can be configured to scale based on metrics such as CPU utilization, HTTP queue length, or custom rules.

```
{
"rules": [
{
"metricTrigger": {
"metricName": "CpuPercentage",
"operator": "GreaterThan",
"threshold": 70,
"timeGrain": "PT1M",
"statistic": "Average",
"timeWindow": "PT5M",
"timeAggregation": "Average"
},
"scaleAction": {
```

```
"direction": "Increase",
"type": "ChangeCount",
"value": "1",
"cooldown": "PT5M"
}
}
]
}
```

Azure Function Elasticity

Azure Functions follow a consumption-based model and are inherently elastic. They scale to zero when idle and can instantly spin up thousands of instances when demand spikes.

This is ideal for workloads such as event processing, API ingestion, or real-time analytics.

Scalability in Databases

A scalable application must be backed by scalable data stores. Azure offers several options depending on your consistency, throughput, and storage requirements.

- **Azure SQL Database**: Scales with elastic pools or hyperscale tier.
- **Cosmos DB**: Offers elastic scalability with global distribution and automatic partitioning.

- **Azure Table Storage**: Suited for massive, low-cost key-value storage.

Cosmos DB Throughput Scaling

Cosmos DB provides auto-scaling throughput (RU/s), ensuring cost efficiency and performance under variable loads.

```
{
"autoscaleSettings": {
"maxThroughput": 4000
}
}
```

With Cosmos DB, developers can avoid over-provisioning and only pay for what is used, while maintaining sub-10ms latencies.

Load Balancing and Scalability

Scalability doesn't function well without proper load distribution. Azure offers various load balancing solutions based on network and application needs.

Service	Type	Use Case
Azure Load Balancer	Layer 4 (TCP/UDP)	Internal services, low-latency apps
Application Gateway	Layer 7 (HTTP/HTTPS)	Web traffic, SSL termination, URL-based routing
Azure Front Door	Global HTTP load balancer	High availability and performance for web apps
Traffic Manager	DNS-based	Geographic routing, failover

These tools ensure incoming traffic is efficiently routed to healthy instances, improving both reliability and performance.

Designing for Scale

Designing applications for scalability involves not only leveraging scalable services but also following architectural practices:

- **Statelessness**: Ensure application components are stateless so they can be replicated without dependency conflicts.
- **Partitioning**: Divide data and processes into segments (e.g., sharding in databases).
- **Asynchronous Communication**: Use queues and pub/sub models to decouple services and improve elasticity.
- **Caching**: Reduce redundant processing by storing frequently accessed data.

Example: Stateless Web App

A stateless app deployed across 3 App Service instances behind an Azure Application Gateway can handle increased traffic efficiently, as each instance performs independently, and user session data is stored in Azure Redis Cache or Cosmos DB.

Cost Implications of Scaling

Scaling affects cost in both directions:

- **Under-scaling** leads to service outages and poor user experience.
- **Over-scaling** results in unnecessary cost.

Azure Cost Management and budgeting tools help monitor and optimize expenses. Azure Advisor provides actionable recommendations for right-sizing resources.

Key strategies include:

- Auto-shutdown of dev/test VMs
- Reserved instances for predictable workloads
- Azure Hybrid Benefit to reduce licensing costs
- Usage of Spot VMs for non-critical workloads

Monitoring and Testing Scalability

To ensure that your system scales correctly under load, you must simulate real-world conditions.

- **Azure Load Testing** helps simulate high traffic to evaluate autoscale behavior.
- **Azure Monitor** and **Application Insights** track metrics like request rates, latencies, and failure counts.
- **Azure Metrics Explorer** allows you to visualize scale-out and scale-in events.

Example: Kusto Query for Scaling Metrics

```
requests
| where timestamp > ago(1h)
| summarize avgDuration=avg(duration), requestCount=count() by bin(timestamp, 5m)
```

Scalability Patterns in Azure

Several design patterns are explicitly designed to address scaling challenges:

- **Queue-Based Load Leveling Pattern**: Smooths traffic spikes by using queues between services.
- **Competing Consumers Pattern**: Enables multiple consumers to process messages in parallel.
- **Throttling Pattern**: Controls resource consumption when demand exceeds capacity.

Each of these can be implemented using Azure-native services such as:

- **Azure Service Bus**
- **Azure Storage Queues**
- **Azure Event Hubs**
- **Azure Functions with Queue Triggers**

Real-World Scenario: News Aggregator Platform

A news aggregation service receives a surge of traffic during breaking news. It uses:

- **Azure Front Door** to route users globally.
- **Azure App Service with Auto-Scale** to handle sudden traffic increases.
- **Azure Functions** to process news feeds asynchronously.
- **Azure Cosmos DB with auto-scale** to store headlines.
- **Azure Redis Cache** to serve popular articles instantly.

Without scalability and elasticity, such a system would either crash or become prohibitively expensive to operate continuously at peak capacity.

Summary

Scalability and elasticity are not optional features—they are the foundation of any modern, cloud-native application. With Azure, these principles can be applied at every layer:

- Compute

- Storage
- Networking
- Data
- Integration

Properly architected systems respond to demand without human intervention, ensure business continuity, and make efficient use of cloud resources. These characteristics are the hallmark of mature, production-grade Azure solutions.

The rest of this book builds on this foundation, showing how to combine scalability with other core principles like availability, security, and performance to create robust cloud architectures.

High Availability and Disaster Recovery

High Availability (HA) and Disaster Recovery (DR) are essential pillars of a resilient cloud architecture. These principles ensure that your applications remain accessible, reliable, and consistent—even in the face of hardware failures, network issues, regional outages, or natural disasters. In Microsoft Azure, HA and DR strategies are supported by a wide range of services and best practices that together help minimize downtime, data loss, and business disruption.

Understanding High Availability

High availability is the ability of a system or application to remain operational and accessible for a high percentage of time, typically quantified as "nines" of availability:

Availability	Downtime per Year
99%	~3.65 days
99.9%	~8.76 hours
99.99%	~52 minutes
99.999%	~5.26 minutes

Achieving high availability involves eliminating single points of failure, using redundant resources, and architecting fault-tolerant systems.

Azure Services for High Availability

Azure provides built-in redundancy and failover mechanisms in most of its core services. Examples include:

- **Availability Sets**: Group of VMs spread across fault and update domains.
- **Availability Zones**: Physically separated datacenters within a region, offering higher isolation.
- **Azure Load Balancer**: Distributes traffic across multiple instances for reliability.
- **Azure Traffic Manager**: Routes traffic to the most responsive or available endpoint.
- **Azure SQL Database**: Built-in high availability with automated failover and geo-replication.

Example: Using Availability Zones with AKS

```
az aks create \
```

—resource-group myResourceGroup \

—name myAKSCluster \

—node-count 3 \

—zones 1 2 3 \

—enable-addons monitoring \

—generate-ssh-keys

This ensures that the nodes are distributed across different availability zones, improving fault tolerance.

Application-Level Redundancy

High availability should also be enforced at the application level:

- **Stateless Microservices**: Easier to scale and restart across multiple zones or regions.
- **Load Balanced Endpoints**: Using Application Gateway or Azure Front Door to distribute requests.
- **Failover Databases**: Azure SQL, Cosmos DB, and PostgreSQL Flexible Server all support automated failover.

Data Replication for HA

High availability also requires data to be replicated across different physical locations. Azure provides this automatically for many services:

- **Azure Storage**:

○ **Locally Redundant Storage (LRS)**: Replicates data within a single data center.

○ **Zone-Redundant Storage (ZRS)**: Replicates across availability zones.

○ **Geo-Redundant Storage (GRS)**: Replicates to a secondary region for disaster recovery.

```
{
"sku": {
"name": "Standard_GRS"
},
"kind": "StorageV2",
"location": "eastus"
}
```

Choosing the right replication strategy depends on your application's RPO (Recovery Point Objective) and RTO (Recovery Time Objective) requirements.

Understanding Disaster Recovery

Disaster Recovery (DR) is the ability to restore operations and data after a catastrophic failure or large-scale outage. While HA aims to avoid downtime, DR prepares for it. DR plans should be clearly documented, tested regularly, and aligned with business continuity goals.

Key Concepts:

- **RPO (Recovery Point Objective)**: The maximum acceptable amount of data loss measured in time.
- **RTO (Recovery Time Objective)**: The target time to restore normal operations after a disruption.

Azure enables DR through replication, backups, failover strategies, and orchestration services.

Azure Services for Disaster Recovery

Service	Role in DR
Azure Site Recovery (ASR)	Replicates on-premises or VM workloads to Azure
Azure Backup	Long-term, secure backups for data and virtual machines
Geo-Replication	Enabled in Azure SQL, Cosmos DB, and Storage
Azure Automation + Runbooks	DR orchestration and runbook execution
Azure Resource Manager (ARM) Templates / Bicep	Declarative redeployment of infrastructure

Example: Configuring Azure Site Recovery

az backup vault create—resource-group myRG—name myVault—location eastus

az backup policy set—vault-name myVault—name myPolicy—backup-management-type AzureIaasVM az backup protection enable-for-vm—vault-name myVault—resource-group myRG—vm myVM

This protects a VM by enabling Azure Backup and assigning a backup policy.

Geo-Disaster Recovery Scenarios

Geo-redundancy is a cornerstone of disaster recovery in the cloud. Azure enables geo-disaster recovery through:

- **Active/Passive Failover**: Primary region handles traffic; secondary is on standby (e.g., SQL Geo-Replication).
- **Active/Active Architectures**: Both regions actively serve traffic (e.g., Azure Front Door with multiple backend regions).
- **Cold Standby**: Infrastructure in secondary region remains off until activated.
- **Warm Standby**: A smaller, operational version of the environment is always running.

These models vary in complexity, cost, and recovery time, allowing you to tailor strategies to your business needs.

Example: Active/Passive for Azure SQL

1. Enable Geo-Replication
2. Configure a failover group
3. Use DNS-based routing or Traffic Manager to redirect clients

```
—T-SQL to add a geo-secondary

ALTER DATABASE [SalesDB] ADD SECONDARY ON SERVER [secondaryserver] AS COPY OF [SalesDB];
```

Testing and Validating HA/DR

You cannot assume that HA and DR work unless you test them. Azure provides several methods for testing failover and simulating outages.

- **Planned Failover**: Validate recovery with minimal risk (e.g., SQL Geo-replication).
- **Chaos Engineering**: Inject faults using Azure Chaos Studio to test resilience.
- **Recovery Drills**: Regular DR simulations using Azure Automation and Site Recovery.
- **Monitoring Tools**: Azure Monitor, Application Insights, and Log Analytics to observe uptime and behavior during failover.

Example: Basic Chaos Experiment with Azure Chaos Studio

```
{
"selectors": [
{
"type": "List",
"targets": [
```

```
"/subscriptions/{subId}/resourceGroups/myRG/providers/
Microsoft.Compute/virtualMachines/myVM"
]
}
],
"steps": [
{
"name": "ShutdownVM",
"actions": [
{
"type": "continuous",
"duration": "PT5M",
"parameters": {
"faultType": "Shutdown"
}
}
]
}
]
}
```

Combining HA and DR into Resilient Design

HA and DR are not mutually exclusive—they must work together. A resilient design embraces both:

- Use **Availability Zones** for local fault tolerance (HA)
- Use **Geo-Replication** for regional disasters (DR)
- Combine **Load Balancer + Traffic Manager** for seamless failover
- Maintain **automated backups** and **IaC deployments** for rapid recovery

The integration of observability (monitoring, logging, tracing) further ensures issues are detected and resolved quickly.

Business Considerations

The technical architecture must align with business requirements and compliance mandates. Considerations include:

- **SLAs**: Match uptime requirements with Azure service-level agreements.
- **Compliance**: Ensure disaster recovery meets regulatory standards (e.g., GDPR, HIPAA).
- **Cost vs. Risk**: Balance investment in redundancy with business impact of downtime.

For example, a healthcare system handling patient data might require hot standby environments and encrypted geo-replication, while a blog might suffice with periodic backups and cold storage.

Summary

High Availability and Disaster Recovery are critical for ensuring business continuity in the cloud. In Azure, these principles are embedded into the platform and supported through a rich ecosystem of tools and services. To implement effective HA/DR strategies, architects must:

- Understand the differences and overlaps between HA and DR
- Leverage Azure-native redundancy features and global distribution
- Implement observability and automation for continuous assurance
- Regularly test and refine failover mechanisms

Cloud-native resilience isn't accidental—it's engineered. And with Azure, it's achievable. The next sections in this book will build on this principle by introducing security, compliance, and cost optimization strategies that make cloud architectures not only resilient but also secure and sustainable.

Security and Compliance in Azure

Security and compliance are foundational pillars in any cloud architecture. In Microsoft Azure, security is not an afterthought or an add-on—it is woven into every layer of the platform. Organizations operating in regulated industries such as finance, healthcare, and government must adhere to strict compliance standards, while all businesses must protect against evolving cyber threats. Azure provides a comprehensive set of services, tools, and practices that enable organizations to meet these needs proactively and effectively.

Security in Azure operates under a **shared responsibility model**, where Microsoft ensures the security of the cloud infrastructure, while customers are responsible for securing their applications, data, and user access.

The Azure Security Landscape

Azure's security architecture encompasses the following key layers:

1. **Physical security**: Protection of data centers.
2. **Infrastructure security**: Protection of compute, storage, and network resources.
3. **Application security**: Securing code, APIs, and integrations.
4. **Identity and access control**: Managing authentication and authorization.
5. **Data protection**: Safeguarding data at rest and in transit.
6. **Monitoring and threat detection**: Real-time awareness of vulnerabilities and incidents.
7. **Compliance**: Adherence to standards such as ISO 27001, HIPAA, GDPR, and FedRAMP.

Each layer contributes to a defense-in-depth strategy that reduces the attack surface and mitigates risk across your cloud environment.

Identity and Access Management (IAM)

IAM is one of the most critical aspects of cloud security. In Azure, this is handled through **Azure Active Directory (Azure AD)**. It supports:

- **Single Sign-On (SSO)** for cloud and on-premises applications
- **Multi-Factor Authentication (MFA)**
- **Role-Based Access Control (RBAC)**
- **Conditional Access Policies**
- **Managed Identities** for secure app-to-app communication

Example: Granting RBAC Permissions

```
az role assignment create \
—assignee user@example.com \
—role "Contributor" \
—scope /subscriptions/00000000-0000-0000-0000-000000000000/resourceGroups/MyResourceGroup
```

This command assigns the Contributor role to a user, scoped to a specific resource group, following the principle of least privilege.

Data Protection

Protecting data both at rest and in transit is essential. Azure provides encryption mechanisms by default:

- **Encryption at Rest** using Azure-managed keys or customer-managed keys (CMK)
- **Encryption in Transit** via TLS 1.2 or higher

- . **Azure Key Vault** for storing secrets, keys, and certificates

Azure Key Vault Example

az keyvault create—name MyKeyVault—resource-group MyResourceGroup—location eastus

az keyvault secret set—vault-name MyKeyVault—name "DbPassword"—value "P@ssw0rd123"

By storing secrets in Key Vault, applications can access them securely without hardcoding sensitive information.

Secure Networking

Azure offers network-level security features to protect against unauthorized access and data leakage:

- **Network Security Groups (NSGs)**: Control inbound/outbound traffic at subnet or NIC level.
- **Application Security Groups (ASGs)**: Group resources logically and apply rules dynamically.
- **Azure Firewall**: Stateful, managed firewall as a service.
- **DDoS Protection**: Automatically enabled Basic tier or configurable Standard tier.
- **Private Link**: Secure access to Azure services over a private endpoint.

Example: NSG Rule to Deny Public SSH Access

```
az network nsg rule create \
—resource-group MyResourceGroup \
—nsg-name MyNSG \
—name Deny-SSH \
—protocol Tcp \
—direction Inbound \
—priority 100 \
—source-address-prefixes '*' \
—source-port-ranges '*' \
—destination-address-prefixes '*' \
—destination-port-ranges 22 \
—access Deny
```

This prevents all public SSH access to VMs, significantly reducing attack exposure.

Secure DevOps (DevSecOps)

Incorporating security into every stage of the development lifecycle is known as DevSecOps. Azure supports this through:

- **Azure DevOps** and **GitHub Actions** for secure CI/CD pipelines
- **Static Code Analysis** tools like SonarCloud

- **Dependency Scanning** to detect vulnerable libraries
- **Infrastructure as Code (IaC)** policies with **Azure Policy**
- **Security Center** for governance and threat prevention

Example: GitHub Action with Secret Injection

```
jobs:

deploy:

runs-on: ubuntu-latest

steps:

- name: Checkout code

uses: actions/checkout@v2

- name: Azure Login

uses: azure/login@v1

with:

creds: ${{ secrets.AZURE_CREDENTIALS }}

- name: Deploy Bicep Template

run: |

az deployment group create \

—resource-group MyResourceGroup \

—template-file main.bicep
```

Secrets are managed via GitHub Secrets and injected securely at runtime.

Monitoring, Logging, and Threat Detection

A secure system must also be observable. Azure provides multiple services to monitor system health, detect anomalies, and respond to threats:

- **Azure Monitor**: Central platform for collecting, analyzing, and acting on telemetry.
- **Log Analytics**: Advanced querying and correlation across logs.
- **Application Insights**: APM (Application Performance Monitoring) for developers.
- **Microsoft Defender for Cloud**: Provides threat detection, security recommendations, and compliance insights.
- **Sentinel**: Azure's cloud-native SIEM solution for security incident response.

Example: KQL Query to Detect Unusual Logins

```
SigninLogs
| where ResultType == 0
| summarize count() by UserPrincipalName, bin(TimeGenerated, 1h)
| order by count_ desc
```

This can detect spikes in login attempts and help identify potentially compromised accounts.

Compliance and Governance

Azure is compliant with more than 90 regulatory standards across different industries and geographies, including:

- **ISO 27001, 27017, 27018**
- **SOC 1, 2, 3**
- **GDPR**
- **HIPAA**
- **FedRAMP**

Azure Policy and **Blueprints** allow organizations to define guardrails that ensure compliance across subscriptions and environments.

Example: Enforcing Tags on Resources with Azure Policy

```
{
"if": {
"not": {
"field": "tags",
"exists": "true"
}
},
```

```
"then": {
"effect": "deny"
}
}
```

This policy ensures that all resources have tags, which is critical for cost tracking, ownership, and governance.

Security Best Practices in Azure

1. **Use MFA for all accounts.**
2. **Restrict access with RBAC and Conditional Access.**
3. **Secure secrets using Azure Key Vault.**
4. **Segment networks using NSGs, ASGs, and Firewalls.**
5. **Encrypt everything—at rest and in transit.**
6. **Monitor continuously with Azure Monitor and Defender.**
7. **Automate and test security controls using IaC.**
8. **Keep your dependencies and runtimes patched.**
9. **Apply zero-trust principles: verify explicitly, use least privilege, and assume breach.**
10. **Run regular compliance scans and audits.**

Real-World Scenario: Securing a Multi-Tenant SaaS App

Imagine a multi-tenant SaaS platform hosted on Azure, serving healthcare organizations. The architecture involves:

- Azure Front Door with Web Application Firewall (WAF)

- Azure App Service for API hosting
- Azure SQL Database with row-level security
- Azure AD B2C for user identity
- Azure Key Vault for secrets
- Azure Monitor and Defender for Cloud for visibility

Security implementations include:

- Using **Managed Identity** for services to access Key Vault without credentials.
- Enabling **Private Endpoints** to restrict public access to databases.
- Applying **Conditional Access** policies to restrict admin logins to corporate IP ranges.
- Encrypting all patient data using **customer-managed keys (CMK)**.
- Using **Azure Policy** to enforce tagging, region restrictions, and secure configurations.

The result is a robust, secure, and compliant system that meets both operational needs and regulatory mandates.

Summary

Security and compliance are not optional—they are critical enablers of trust, reliability, and operational excellence in cloud computing. Microsoft Azure offers a powerful ecosystem of tools, services, and practices that help you build secure, compliant, and resilient systems from the ground up.

By mastering identity management, data protection, secure networking, DevSecOps practices, monitoring, and compliance enforcement, you can design and operate systems that meet the highest standards of security and governance.

The next section explores cost optimization—ensuring that all of this security and scalability is achieved without waste, helping your architecture remain sustainable as it grows.

Cost Optimization Strategies

Effective cloud architecture must be not only secure, scalable, and highly available—but also cost-efficient. As organizations scale their workloads in Microsoft Azure, cloud costs can escalate rapidly if not managed with discipline. Cost optimization is about making informed architectural, operational, and service choices that minimize expenditure while maintaining performance, availability, and security.

In Azure, cost optimization is supported by platform-native tools, pricing models, architectural patterns, and best practices. By understanding the various cost levers and implementing proactive monitoring and governance, teams can deliver high-performing solutions without overprovisioning or incurring unnecessary costs.

Understanding the Azure Pricing Model

Azure follows a pay-as-you-go (PAYG) model, where you are billed based on actual consumption of resources. However, the pricing model varies depending on the resource type:

- **Compute**: Based on VM size, operating system, and duration (per-second or per-minute).
- **Storage**: Based on type (Blob, File, Queue), access tier (Hot, Cool, Archive), and redundancy (LRS, ZRS, GRS).
- **Networking**: Based on data transfer (intra-region is often free, outbound is charged).
- **Databases**: Based on DTUs (Database Transaction Units) or vCores, plus storage and backup costs.

Understanding these models is the first step toward optimizing them.

Azure Cost Management and Billing Tools

Azure provides several tools to help you monitor, manage, and reduce your cloud spending:

- **Azure Cost Management + Billing**: Central dashboard to track costs and forecast future spending.
- **Azure Pricing Calculator**: Estimate costs before provisioning resources.
- **Azure Advisor**: Personalized recommendations for cost, performance, reliability, and security.
- **Budgets and Alerts**: Define limits and receive notifications before overspending.
- **Tags**: Categorize resources by owner, environment, or cost center for chargeback/showback.

Example: Creating a Budget in Azure

```
az consumption budget create \
—resource-group MyResourceGroup \
—amount 500 \
—time-grain monthly \
—name DevTeamBudget \
—category cost \
—start-date 2024-01-01 \
—end-date 2024-12-31
```

This creates a budget to ensure that a development team doesn't exceed a set monthly threshold.

Right-Sizing Resources

Overprovisioning is one of the most common causes of cloud waste. Right-sizing involves matching resources to actual usage patterns.

Examples:

- **Virtual Machines**: Choose a size that matches your CPU and memory usage. Consider using burstable B-series VMs for infrequent workloads.
- **App Services**: Scale-down tiers during low-traffic hours (e.g., dev/test environments).
- **Databases**: Switch from provisioned throughput to **serverless** or **elastic pools** where usage is variable.

Example: Using Serverless Azure SQL

```
az sql db create \
—resource-group MyResourceGroup \
—server myserver \
—name mydb \
—edition GeneralPurpose \
—compute-model Serverless \
—auto-pause-delay 60 \
—min-capacity 0.5 \
—max-capacity 4
```

This creates a serverless database that automatically scales based on workload and pauses during inactivity.

Leverage Auto-Scaling and Elastic Models

Auto-scaling not only improves performance but also optimizes cost by reducing idle resources. Azure supports scaling in several services:

- **App Services**: Scale-out based on CPU, memory, or custom metrics.
- **Azure Kubernetes Service (AKS)**: Cluster Autoscaler and Horizontal Pod Autoscaler.
- **Azure Functions**: Consumption plan only incurs cost when code is executed.

- **Virtual Machine Scale Sets**: Automatically adjust VM instances based on demand.

Always pair auto-scaling with monitoring to fine-tune rules and avoid cost surprises.

Use Azure Reservations and Hybrid Benefits

Azure offers substantial discounts for predictable workloads:

- **Reserved Instances (RI)**: Commit to a 1- or 3-year term for VMs, SQL, Cosmos DB, etc., and receive up to 72% discount.

- **Azure Hybrid Benefit**: Use your on-prem Windows Server or SQL Server licenses to reduce VM and SQL costs.

Example: Purchasing a Reserved Instance

You can purchase via the Azure portal or CLI for eligible resources. The process includes selecting region, size, term, and payment plan.

Storage Tiering and Lifecycle Management

Data storage can become a silent budget killer. Azure Blob Storage offers multiple access tiers:

Tier	Intended Usage	Cost
Hot	Frequent access	Highest
Cool	Infrequent access	Lower
Archive	Rarely accessed	Lowest

Use **Lifecycle Management Rules** to transition data between tiers automatically.

Example: Blob Lifecycle Policy

```
{
"rules": [
{
"name": "archive-old-blobs",
"enabled": true,
"type": "Lifecycle",
"definition": {
"actions": {
"baseBlob": {
"tierToCool": { "daysAfterModificationGreaterThan": 30 },
"tierToArchive": { "daysAfterModificationGreaterThan": 90 }
}
},
"filters": {
"blobTypes": [ "blockBlob" ],
"prefixMatch": [ "logs/" ]
}
}
}
```

```
]
}
```

This rule automatically archives blobs in the logs/ folder after 90 days.

Decommission and Deallocate Unused Resources

Idle resources often go unnoticed, especially in non-production environments. Use automation to identify and clean up:

- **Unattached disks**
- **Stopped VMs still incurring charges**
- **Expired snapshots and backups**
- **Unused public IPs**

Script Example: List Unattached Disks

```
az disk list—query "[?managedBy==null].{name:name, resourceGroup:resourceGroup}"—output table
```

This helps identify disks that are incurring storage costs but not attached to any VM.

Optimize Networking Costs

While inbound data is free, outbound data incurs charges. Consider these strategies:

- **Use Content Delivery Network (CDN)** to cache static content close to users.

- **Minimize cross-region data flows.**
- **Use ExpressRoute** for predictable large data transfers.
- **Use Azure Private Link** instead of public IPs for inter-service communication.

Tagging and Chargeback Strategies

Implementing tagging standards helps identify cost ownership and improve accountability. Standard tags include:

- Environment: Production, Staging, Dev
- Owner: User or team name
- CostCenter: Department or billing code
- Project: Internal initiative or client

Azure Policy can enforce the use of tags at deployment.

Example: Enforcing Tag Requirement

```
{
"if": {
"field": "[concat('tags[', parameters('tagName'), ']')]",
"exists": "false"
},
"then": {
```

```
"effect": "deny"
}
}
```

This ensures resources cannot be deployed without the required cost-tracking tags.

Real-World Scenario: Optimizing a FinTech Analytics Platform

A FinTech startup collects transaction data and provides real-time dashboards using Azure. Over time, their costs balloon due to:

- Overprovisioned VMs running 24/7
- Large volumes of unused telemetry in Application Insights
- Always-on databases with erratic usage patterns
- Infrequently accessed logs in Hot Blob storage

Optimization Actions:

- Replaced VMs with Azure Functions for infrequent jobs
- Switched to serverless SQL and Cosmos DB with autoscaling
- Implemented lifecycle management to move old logs to Archive

- Scheduled auto-shutdown for dev environments via Logic Apps
- Purchased 3-year Reserved Instances for production compute

The result: a 47% reduction in monthly Azure spend without sacrificing performance or uptime.

Summary

Cost optimization is not a one-time event—it's a continuous practice of measurement, evaluation, and refinement. In Azure, successful cost management requires a blend of architecture, automation, and awareness.

Key takeaways:

- Understand and apply the right pricing models.
- Use auto-scaling and serverless where possible.
- Right-size and decommission unused resources.
- Leverage reserved pricing and licensing benefits.
- Implement tagging and budgets for governance.
- Continuously monitor and optimize using Azure-native tools.

By integrating these strategies into your architecture and operations, you ensure that your cloud investments are both sustainable and value-driven—paving the way for long-term success.

Chapter 3: Foundational Azure Services

Compute Services: VMs, App Services, and Functions

Compute is the backbone of any cloud application. In Microsoft Azure, compute services provide the ability to run application code, process workloads, execute business logic, and manage background tasks. Azure offers a rich variety of compute options, allowing you to choose the best fit for your application's performance, scalability, and cost requirements.

This section explores the three foundational compute services in Azure: **Virtual Machines (VMs)**, **App Services**, and **Azure Functions**. Each service addresses specific use cases, supports different levels of control, and fits within distinct architectural models.

Virtual Machines (VMs)

Azure Virtual Machines provide Infrastructure as a Service (IaaS), giving users complete control over the operating system, installed software, and configuration. VMs are ideal for applications requiring legacy support, custom runtimes, or specialized environments.

Key Features:

- Full administrative control
- Windows and Linux OS support
- Custom images and extensions

- Integration with Azure Backup and Site Recovery
- Vertical and horizontal scaling

Use Cases:

- Running legacy enterprise applications
- Hosting databases and middleware
- Lifting and shifting on-prem workloads
- Development and testing environments

Provisioning an Azure VM

You can create a VM using the Azure Portal, CLI, or Infrastructure as Code.

```
az vm create \
—resource-group MyResourceGroup \
—name MyVM \
—image UbuntuLTS \
—admin-username azureuser \
—generate-ssh-keys
```

This example provisions a Linux VM with SSH access. You can attach storage, configure networking, and install software as needed.

Scaling VMs

- **Manual Scaling**: Resize the VM or increase the instance count in a scale set.
- **Auto-Scaling**: Use Virtual Machine Scale Sets (VMSS) to dynamically adjust capacity.

```
az vmss create \
—resource-group MyResourceGroup \
—name MyScaleSet \
—image UbuntuLTS \
—upgrade-policy-mode automatic \
—custom-data cloud-init.txt
```

Azure App Services

Azure App Service is a Platform as a Service (PaaS) offering for hosting web applications, RESTful APIs, and mobile backends. It abstracts the infrastructure, allowing developers to focus on building and deploying code.

Key Features:

- Support for .NET, Node.js, Python, Java, PHP, and more
- Built-in CI/CD integration with GitHub, Azure DevOps, Bitbucket

- Auto-scaling and load balancing
- SSL certificates and custom domains
- Integrated diagnostics and Application Insights

Use Cases:

- Enterprise web portals and websites
- Backend APIs for mobile and web apps
- Lightweight CMS systems
- Single Page Applications (SPAs)

Creating an App Service

```
az appservice plan create \
—name MyAppPlan \
—resource-group MyResourceGroup \
—sku S1 \
—is-linux

az webapp create \
—resource-group MyResourceGroup \
—plan MyAppPlan \
—name my-unique-app-name \
—runtime "NODE|18-lts" \
```

—deployment-local-git

This creates an App Service using the Linux plan and deploys a Node.js application.

Scaling App Services

App Services can scale based on CPU, memory, or custom rules:

- **Scale Out**: Add instances
- **Scale Up**: Upgrade to a more powerful pricing tier

Auto-scaling can be configured via the Azure Portal or ARM templates.

Azure Functions

Azure Functions is a serverless compute service that allows you to run code in response to events without managing infrastructure. It operates on a pay-per-execution model, offering cost-effective scalability for event-driven workloads.

Key Features:

- Event-based triggers (HTTP, Timer, Queue, Blob, Event Hub)
- Supports multiple languages: C#, JavaScript, Python, PowerShell
- Consumption-based and Premium plans

- Integration with Azure Logic Apps, Event Grid, and Service Bus
- Built-in monitoring via Application Insights

Use Cases:

- Serverless APIs
- Real-time file or data processing
- Scheduled tasks and CRON jobs
- Backend logic for IoT and chatbots

Creating a Function App

```
az functionapp create \
—resource-group MyResourceGroup \
—consumption-plan-location westus \
—runtime node \
—runtime-version 18 \
—functions-version 4 \
—name myUniqueFunctionApp \
—storage-account mystorageacct
```

This example creates a Node.js-based function app on the consumption plan.

Sample JavaScript Function

```
module.exports = async function (context, req) {
context.log('HTTP trigger received');
const name = req.query.name || (req.body && req.body.name);
const responseMessage = name
? `Hello, ${name}.`
: 'Please pass a name in the query string or in the request body.';
context.res = {
status: 200,
body: responseMessage,
};
};
```

This function can be triggered by an HTTP GET or POST request and demonstrates the simplicity of serverless development.

Comparing Compute Services

Feature	Virtual Machines	App Service	Azure Functions
Model	IaaS	PaaS	Serverless / FaaS
Use Case	Full control needed	Web/API apps	Event-driven processing
Scaling	Manual/VMSS	Auto-scale by plan	Auto-scale by invocation
OS Management	Yes	No	No
Cost Model	Per-hour	Tiered plan	Per-execution
Language Support	Any	Multi-language	Multi-language
CI/CD Support	Manual or scripted	Built-in integrations	Azure DevOps/ GitHub
Monitoring	Log Analytics	App Insights	App Insights

Best Practices for Compute Services

1. **Start with Managed Services**: Use App Services or Functions unless full control is essential.
2. **Right-Size Resources**: Choose the correct SKU and pricing tier based on load and usage.
3. **Separate Workloads**: Isolate long-running, CPU-bound, and memory-intensive processes.
4. **Secure Access**: Use Managed Identities and restrict access via NSGs and Private Endpoints.
5. **Implement Observability**: Always monitor compute resources for health, performance, and usage.
6. **Use IaC for Consistency**: Deploy compute services with ARM, Bicep, or Terraform templates.

Real-World Scenario: E-Commerce Platform

An e-commerce company is building a cloud-native architecture using multiple Azure compute options:

- **Front-End**: React application hosted via Azure Static Web Apps
- **API Gateway**: Azure API Management
- **Backend Services**:
  - Azure App Services for core business logic
  - Azure Functions for order confirmations and notifications
  - Azure VMs for legacy billing engine (to be containerized later)

Benefits of this hybrid compute model:

- Cost-effective scaling for unpredictable workloads (Functions)
- Simplified DevOps pipelines for APIs (App Services)
- Gradual migration of legacy apps (VMs to AKS or Containers)
- Centralized security and routing (API Management)

Summary

Compute services in Azure offer a spectrum of control, flexibility, and abstraction:

- **Virtual Machines** provide the most control but require active management.
- **App Services** abstract infrastructure and enable rapid deployment of web apps and APIs.
- **Azure Functions** allow you to write event-driven code with zero infrastructure concerns.

Choosing the right compute option—and combining them wisely—is critical to building scalable, cost-efficient, and maintainable Azure solutions. This foundational understanding sets the stage for exploring storage, networking, and identity services in the next sections.

Storage Options: Blob, Table, Queue, and File

Storage is a critical component of any cloud-native application. In Azure, storage services are designed to meet a wide range of needs—from handling massive unstructured data lakes to delivering low-latency message queues and high-performance file shares. Each Azure storage offering is optimized for specific types of data and access patterns, enabling you to architect resilient, scalable, and cost-effective solutions.

This section covers the foundational Azure storage services: **Blob Storage**, **Table Storage**, **Queue Storage**, and **File Storage**. Together, they form the core of **Azure Storage Account** capabilities, which provide unified management, security, and redundancy features.

Azure Storage Account Overview

An Azure Storage Account is a container for multiple types of storage services. It provides:

- A unique namespace in Azure
- Support for multiple data types (blob, file, queue, table)
- Redundancy and replication options (LRS, ZRS, GRS, RA-GRS)
- Secure access through Shared Access Signatures (SAS), Azure AD, or connection strings
- Monitoring and metrics integration with Azure Monitor

```
az storage account create \
—name mystorageaccount \
—resource-group MyResourceGroup \
—location eastus \
—sku Standard_LRS \
—kind StorageV2
```

Blob Storage

Blob (Binary Large Object) Storage is designed for storing massive amounts of unstructured data such as images, videos, documents, and backups.

Tiers

Azure Blob Storage supports three access tiers:

- **Hot**: Optimized for frequent access.
- **Cool**: Lower cost for infrequent access.
- **Archive**: Ultra-low cost for rarely accessed data.

These tiers can be applied at the blob or container level and transitioned automatically via lifecycle rules.

Types of Blobs

- **Block Blobs**: Ideal for most files (text, images, etc.)
- **Append Blobs**: Optimized for append operations (e.g., logs)
- **Page Blobs**: Used primarily for Azure VM disks

Sample: Uploading a File to Blob

az storage blob upload \

—account-name mystorageaccount \

—container-name mycontainer \

—name image.jpg \

—file ./image.jpg

Use Cases

- Storing media for web apps
- Backup and disaster recovery
- Logging and telemetry
- Data lakes for analytics

Table Storage

Azure Table Storage is a NoSQL key-value store optimized for fast read/write access to large volumes of data.

Structure

- Tables are collections of entities.
- Each entity has properties (key-value pairs).
- Entities are indexed by **PartitionKey** and **RowKey**.

This structure supports high scalability and is ideal for scenarios where relational models are not required.

Sample: Inserting a Table Entity

az storage entity insert \

—account-name mystorageaccount \

—table-name Users \

—entity PartitionKey=Customer RowKey=12345 Name=John Age=34

Use Cases

- User profiles and device metadata
- Configuration data
- Audit and event logs
- Lightweight CMS backends

Queue Storage

Azure Queue Storage provides simple messaging for cloud-based applications. It allows components to communicate asynchronously, enabling better decoupling and scalability.

Key Concepts

- Queues hold messages.
- Messages are typically up to 64KB (max ~7 days retention).
- Producers send messages; consumers read/delete messages.

This is especially powerful for load-leveling and retry patterns in microservices and distributed systems.

Sample: Sending a Queue Message

az storage message put \

—account-name mystorageaccount \

—queue-name myqueue \

—content "Process order 12345"

Use Cases

- Background job management
- Decoupling web frontends and processing backends
- Task scheduling
- Retry and fault-tolerant patterns

File Storage

Azure File Storage provides fully managed file shares in the cloud, accessible via SMB and NFS protocols.

Features

- Fully managed, serverless
- Can be mounted by Windows, Linux, or macOS

- Supports file-level access control
- Integration with Azure File Sync for hybrid deployments

Sample: Mounting File Share on Linux

sudo mount -t cifs //mystorageaccount.file.core.windows.net/myshare /mnt/myshare \

-o

vers=3.0,username=mystorageaccount,password=yourkey,dir_mode=07

Use Cases

- Lift-and-shift enterprise file shares
- Container shared volumes
- Application configuration and runtime file access
- Hosting legacy software installers or assets

Choosing the Right Storage Option

Requirement	Recommended Service	Notes
Store media, logs, backups	Blob Storage	Use Hot/Cool/Archive tiers based on access frequency
Key-value data	Table Storage	Best for semi-structured or unstructured NoSQL workloads
Asynchronous communication	Queue Storage	Enables decoupled, distributed systems
Shared file access	File Storage	SMB/NFS accessible; works well in hybrid environments

Security and Access Control

Azure Storage supports multiple mechanisms to secure data:

- **Encryption at Rest**: Enabled by default with Microsoft-managed or customer-managed keys.
- **Encryption in Transit**: Enforced via HTTPS.
- **Identity-Based Access**: Azure AD-based RBAC or Shared Access Signature (SAS).
- **Private Endpoints**: Restrict access over private IPs within a VNet.

Example: Generating a SAS Token

```
az storage blob generate-sas \
—account-name mystorageaccount \
```

```
—container-name mycontainer \
—name report.pdf \
—permissions r \
—expiry 2025-01-01T00:00Z
```

Monitoring and Metrics

Azure Storage integrates with:

- **Azure Monitor**: For metrics like ingress, egress, latency
- **Activity Log**: Tracks management operations
- **Diagnostic Settings**: Logs read/write/delete operations
- **Log Analytics**: Query and analyze storage activity

Example: KQL Query for Blob Read Operations

```
AzureDiagnostics
| where ResourceType == "STORAGEACCOUNTS" and OperationName == "GetBlob"
| summarize count() by TimeGenerated, AccountName
```

Advanced Concepts

- **Data Lifecycle Management**: Automate blob tiering and deletion.

- **Immutable Blobs**: Set legal holds and time-based retention (compliance use cases).
- **Change Feed**: Track changes to blobs for auditing or analytics.
- **Event Grid Integration**: React to blob creation/deletion with serverless triggers.

Real-World Scenario: Content Delivery and Archival

A media company stores thousands of videos and metadata records. Their architecture uses:

- **Blob Storage (Hot)** for frequently streamed content
- **Blob Storage (Archive)** for long-term retention
- **Table Storage** for storing metadata like titles, categories, and ratings
- **Queue Storage** to trigger video encoding jobs via Azure Functions
- **Azure CDN** for low-latency content delivery to global audiences

This results in a scalable, cost-effective storage solution capable of handling millions of daily requests.

Summary

Azure's storage services provide the flexibility to support any data access pattern or application workload. From unstructured files and multimedia to structured NoSQL entities and asynchronous messages, these foundational services form the backbone of modern cloud architectures.

Key takeaways:

- **Blob Storage** is ideal for large, unstructured objects with tiered access.
- **Table Storage** supports fast, scalable access to key-value data.
- **Queue Storage** enables distributed system communication and decoupling.
- **File Storage** brings familiar file system access to the cloud.

Choosing the right storage service—and using it with appropriate security, redundancy, and automation—ensures your applications are robust, scalable, and efficient. The next section will build on this foundation by exploring networking essentials that enable secure, performant, and interconnected cloud services.

Networking Essentials: VNets, Gateways, and Load Balancers

Networking is the circulatory system of any cloud architecture. In Microsoft Azure, networking services provide the foundation for securely connecting and managing application components, users, and systems. Whether you're deploying a simple web app or a complex multi-tier enterprise solution, understanding Azure's networking fundamentals is critical to building performant, scalable, and secure applications.

This section explores the key networking building blocks in Azure—**Virtual Networks (VNets)**, **Gateways**, and **Load Balancers**. These components enable you to define private address spaces, route traffic, enforce isolation, and ensure high availability for your services.

Azure Virtual Network (VNet)

An Azure Virtual Network (VNet) is a logically isolated segment of the Azure cloud dedicated to your subscription. It acts like a traditional network in an on-premises data center but with enhanced scalability, flexibility, and integration with Azure services.

Key Features:

- IP address management using CIDR blocks
- Subnetting for segmentation
- Route tables and Network Security Groups (NSGs)
- Peering for VNet-to-VNet communication
- Private endpoints to securely access PaaS services

Creating a VNet with Subnets

az network vnet create \

—resource-group MyResourceGroup \

—name MyVNet \

—address-prefix 10.0.0.0/16 \

—subnet-name WebSubnet \

—subnet-prefix 10.0.1.0/24

This command creates a VNet with a single subnet. Additional subnets can be added to isolate database, backend, and other components.

Subnet Segmentation and Security

Subnets are used to divide the VNet into smaller segments. This enables role-based access control and traffic restrictions.

- **Frontend Subnet**: Hosts publicly accessible components (e.g., web apps).
- **Backend Subnet**: Contains databases, APIs, or sensitive data.
- **Jumpbox Subnet**: Hosts bastion hosts or admin VMs for secure access.

Apply **Network Security Groups (NSGs)** to subnets to control inbound and outbound traffic:

az network nsg rule create \

—resource-group MyResourceGroup \

—nsg-name BackendNSG \

—name AllowSQL \

—priority 100 \

—direction Inbound \

—access Allow \

—protocol Tcp \

—source-address-prefixes 10.0.1.0/24 \

—destination-port-ranges 1433

This example allows SQL traffic from a specific subnet.

VNet Peering

VNet Peering enables private, low-latency communication between VNets—either in the same or different regions.

Use Cases:

- Connecting app and database VNets
- Multi-region failover
- Separation of environments (dev/test/prod)

az network vnet peering create \

—name AppToDbPeering \

—resource-group MyResourceGroup \

—vnet-name AppVNet \

—remote-vnet DbVNet \

—allow-vnet-access

Peering is transitive within regions but not across them unless configured explicitly.

Gateways in Azure Networking

Azure provides several types of gateways to connect your VNet with other networks, both in Azure and on-premises.

VPN Gateway

Enables secure, encrypted tunnels between Azure VNets and on-premises networks.

- **Route-based** (dynamic routing) or **policy-based**
- Supports **Point-to-Site**, **Site-to-Site**, and **VNet-to-VNet** connections
- Common protocols: IKEv2, OpenVPN

ExpressRoute Gateway

Provides private, dedicated connectivity from on-premises to Azure via a telecom provider. It bypasses the public internet for enhanced reliability and security.

- Supports higher bandwidth (up to 10 Gbps)
- SLA-backed availability
- Integration with private peering, Microsoft peering, and public peering

Application Gateway

Layer 7 load balancer that supports SSL termination, URL-based routing, and Web Application Firewall (WAF).

Azure Bastion

A secure way to access VMs via RDP/SSH without exposing public IPs.

```
az network bastion create \
—name MyBastion \
—resource-group MyResourceGroup \
—vnet-name MyVNet \
—public-ip-address MyBastionIP \
—location eastus
```

Load Balancing Options

Load balancing in Azure is essential for distributing traffic across multiple servers or services to improve performance and availability.

Azure Load Balancer (Layer 4)

- Distributes TCP/UDP traffic at the transport layer
- Used for internal and external load balancing
- Offers health probes to monitor endpoint availability

Application Gateway (Layer 7)

- HTTP/HTTPS-based load balancing
- URL path-based routing

- Cookie affinity and SSL offloading
- WAF for protecting web applications

Azure Front Door

- Global load balancer with edge network acceleration
- Smart routing and geo-redundancy
- SSL offload and custom domain HTTPS

Azure Traffic Manager

- DNS-based global load balancing
- Supports geographic routing, latency routing, and failover
- Used to distribute traffic between multiple Azure regions

Load Balancer Configuration Example

az network lb create \

—resource-group MyResourceGroup \

—name MyLoadBalancer \

—frontend-ip-name MyFrontEnd \

—backend-pool-name MyBackEndPool \

—public-ip-address MyPublicIP

To add health probes:

```
az network lb probe create \
—resource-group MyResourceGroup \
—lb-name MyLoadBalancer \
—name MyHealthProbe \
—protocol tcp \
—port 80
```

Private Endpoints and Private Link

To access Azure PaaS services (e.g., Azure SQL, Blob Storage) over a private IP address:

- **Private Link** creates private endpoints within a VNet
- Reduces exposure to the public internet
- Increases security and compliance

Creating a Private Endpoint

```
az network private-endpoint create \
—name MyPrivateEndpoint \
—resource-group MyResourceGroup \
—vnet-name MyVNet \
—subnet MySubnet \
```

```
—private-connection-resource-id
"/subscriptions/.../resourceGroups/.../providers/Microsoft.Sql/servers/mySqlServer" \

—group-ids sqlServer \

—connection-name MySqlPrivateConnection
```

Monitoring and Diagnostics

Azure networking services are tightly integrated with monitoring tools:

- **Azure Network Watcher**: Provides topology, flow logs, and connection troubleshooting
- **Diagnostic Settings**: Export logs to Log Analytics, Event Hubs, or Storage
- **Connection Monitor**: End-to-end network performance testing
- **Traffic Analytics**: Gain insights into NSG flows

Example: NSG Flow Logs to Log Analytics

```
az network watcher flow-log configure \

—resource-group MyResourceGroup \

—nsg MyNSG \

—enabled true \

—log-analytics-workspace MyWorkspace
```

Best Practices

1. **Segment your network**: Use subnets and NSGs to isolate workloads.
2. **Restrict public IPs**: Use Bastion and Private Link for secure access.
3. **Use managed gateways**: Prefer Azure VPN or ExpressRoute over DIY tunnels.
4. **Apply least privilege**: Secure routing and firewall rules with precision.
5. **Implement redundancy**: Use Load Balancer, Front Door, or Traffic Manager for HA.
6. **Encrypt everything**: Ensure TLS is used end-to-end.
7. **Monitor continuously**: Set up alerts and diagnostics on all networking components.

Real-World Scenario: Multi-Region Enterprise Web App

A global enterprise deploys a multi-region web application architecture:

- **App Tier**: Hosted in App Services behind Application Gateway (with WAF)
- **Data Tier**: Azure SQL with geo-replication between regions
- **Networking**:
  - VNet with subnets for app, data, and monitoring
  - NSGs applied to restrict traffic

○ Azure Front Door to route global traffic and ensure failover

○ VPN Gateway connected to the on-premises datacenter

○ Azure Bastion for admin VM access without public IPs

This setup ensures high availability, data sovereignty, and secure connectivity across the globe.

Summary

Networking in Azure is vast and powerful, offering the tools to build secure, resilient, and globally distributed applications. Whether you're enabling private connectivity, securing traffic, balancing loads, or linking multiple regions, Azure networking services provide everything needed to construct a robust network fabric.

Key takeaways:

- **VNets** form the foundation of private cloud networking.
- **Subnets and NSGs** enforce security and traffic segmentation.
- **Gateways** extend connectivity beyond Azure.
- **Load balancers and Front Door** ensure availability and performance.
- **Private Link and Bastion** enhance security and compliance.

A strong grasp of these essentials enables cloud architects and developers to build connected solutions that are scalable, secure, and performant by design. The next section will explore Azure's identity and access management services—essential for protecting your applications and data.

Azure Identity and Access Management

Identity is the cornerstone of security in cloud computing. In Microsoft Azure, **Identity and Access Management (IAM)** provides the foundation for securing resources, enforcing least privilege, enabling secure application access, and complying with regulatory requirements. Azure implements IAM through a robust and extensible system that centers around **Azure Active Directory (Azure AD)** and integrates seamlessly with virtually every Azure service.

This section explores how Azure handles identity, authentication, and authorization. It introduces key concepts such as **Azure AD**, **Role-Based Access Control (RBAC)**, **Conditional Access**, **Managed Identities**, and **Privileged Identity Management (PIM)**. Together, these elements form a powerful, enterprise-ready identity management ecosystem.

Azure Active Directory (Azure AD)

Azure AD is Microsoft's cloud-based identity and access management service. It is used for:

- Authenticating users, services, and devices
- Authorizing access to applications and resources

- Supporting single sign-on (SSO) across Microsoft 365, SaaS apps, and custom applications
- Enabling secure federation with on-premises directories

Azure AD vs Azure AD B2C vs Azure AD B2B

Feature	Azure AD	Azure AD B2C	Azure AD B2B
Target Users	Employees	Customers and citizens	Partners and contractors
Authentication	Internal directory	Custom-branded identity	External identities
Federation	Supported	Supported	Supported
Use Cases	Enterprise IT	SaaS applications, portals	Cross-org collaboration

Authentication in Azure

Authentication is the process of verifying identity. Azure AD supports several authentication mechanisms:

- **Username + Password**
- **Multi-Factor Authentication (MFA)**
- **Passwordless Authentication** (biometrics, FIDO2, authenticator app)
- **OAuth 2.0 and OpenID Connect** for web and mobile apps
- **SAML and WS-Federation** for legacy apps

- **Certificates and client secrets** for service-to-service access

Example: Azure AD OAuth 2.0 Authorization Flow

1. Application redirects user to Azure AD login page.
2. User authenticates with username/password and optional MFA.
3. Azure AD issues an **ID token** (identity) and an **access token** (resource access).
4. Application uses the access token to call Azure APIs or custom backends.

Role-Based Access Control (RBAC)

RBAC allows fine-grained control over Azure resources by assigning **roles** to **users, groups, or service principals** at different scopes (subscription, resource group, or individual resource).

Built-in Roles

- **Owner**: Full management, including access
- **Contributor**: Full management, excluding access
- **Reader**: View-only permissions
- **User Access Administrator**: Manage access permissions

Assigning a Role via CLI

az role assignment create \

—assignee user@example.com \

—role "Contributor" \

—scope /subscriptions/xxxx/resourceGroups/MyResourceGroup

Custom roles can also be defined using JSON policy documents.

Best Practices

- Use **least privilege**: Grant only what is needed.
- Assign roles to **groups** instead of individuals.
- Review access **periodically**.
- Combine RBAC with **Conditional Access** for contextual control.

Conditional Access

Conditional Access (CA) policies enforce access controls based on real-time conditions, such as user location, device state, or risk level.

Common Conditions:

- Sign-in risk (from Identity Protection)
- Device compliance (via Intune)

- Location (IP or geography)
- Application sensitivity
- User roles or groups

Example: Requiring MFA for Admins

1. Target users in the "Administrators" group
2. Require MFA if signing in from outside a trusted network
3. Block access if device is not compliant

Conditional Access enhances security by reducing the reliance on static credentials and applying **adaptive policies** that evolve with threat posture.

Managed Identities

Managed Identities simplify secure access between Azure services by eliminating the need to manage secrets or credentials.

Two types of managed identities:

- **System-assigned**: Tied to a specific Azure resource (e.g., VM, Function)
- **User-assigned**: Standalone identity that can be assigned to multiple resources

Managed Identities work seamlessly with services such as:

- Azure Key Vault
- Azure SQL Database

- Azure Storage
- Azure Event Hubs

Example: Accessing Key Vault with a Managed Identity

1. Assign a system-assigned identity to your Azure Function.
2. Grant that identity permission to read secrets from Key Vault.

```
az keyvault set-policy \
—name MyVault \
—object-id <function-principal-id> \
—secret-permissions get list
```

1. In the function code, use the default credential chain to access secrets without hardcoded keys.

Privileged Identity Management (PIM)

PIM is an Azure AD Premium feature that provides **just-in-time (JIT) elevation** of privileges for sensitive roles.

Features:

- Time-bound role activation
- Approval workflows for role elevation
- MFA enforcement on role activation

- Audit logs and alerts for high-risk access

This minimizes standing access, reducing the attack surface for privileged accounts.

Application Registration and Enterprise Apps

Azure AD allows you to register applications for secure authentication and API access.

App Registration:

- Defines the app's identity and permissions
- Supports authentication flows (e.g., authorization code, client credentials)
- Used for both first-party and third-party apps

Enterprise Applications:

- Represents configured apps available to users
- Supports SSO and Conditional Access

Sample App Registration via CLI

```
az ad app create \
—display-name "MyApp" \
—identifier-uris "https://myapp.example.com" \
—reply-urls "https://myapp.example.com/auth" \
```

—available-to-other-tenants false

Monitoring and Auditing IAM

Identity-related activities must be continuously monitored to detect anomalies and maintain compliance.

Azure provides:

- **Sign-in Logs**: Capture authentication attempts and results
- **Audit Logs**: Track changes to identities, roles, and policies
- **Identity Protection**: Detects risky users and sign-ins
- **Azure Monitor and Log Analytics**: Enable alerting and dashboarding

KQL: Sign-ins from Unknown Locations

```
SigninLogs

| where LocationDetails.countryOrRegion != "United States"

| summarize count() by UserPrincipalName, LocationDetails
```

Set alerts on unusual patterns, failed logins, or high-risk sign-ins.

Real-World Scenario: Securing a SaaS Platform

A SaaS company builds a multi-tenant platform on Azure with strict identity requirements:

- Azure AD B2C for external customer logins with social and email providers
- RBAC for admin users managing tenant configurations
- Conditional Access policies for back-office apps requiring MFA
- Managed Identities for secure API calls between Azure Functions and Azure SQL
- PIM for engineering leads to elevate to Owner during production incidents

This architecture enforces security and compliance while maintaining usability and scalability.

Summary

Identity is the new perimeter in the cloud. Azure's Identity and Access Management services empower organizations to secure their applications, control access to resources, and comply with regulatory standards without compromising agility.

Key takeaways:

- **Azure AD** is the control plane for authentication and authorization.
- **RBAC** ensures fine-grained, scoped access to resources.
- **Conditional Access** adapts security in real time based on context.

- **Managed Identities** eliminate secrets in service-to-service communication.
- **Privileged Identity Management** reduces standing access and improves auditability.

As your Azure environment scales, so does the complexity of identity. Investing in a strong IAM strategy from day one ensures secure, maintainable, and compliant cloud operations. The next chapter will explore architectural design patterns that bring all these foundational services together in structured, repeatable ways.

Chapter 4: Architectural Design Patterns in Azure

The Microservices Pattern

The microservices architectural pattern is a modern, flexible approach to building distributed applications. It emphasizes breaking down applications into small, independently deployable services, each responsible for a specific business capability. In Azure, microservices architecture is not just a theoretical model—it's a practical reality enabled by a powerful suite of services including Azure Kubernetes Service (AKS), Azure Container Apps, Azure API Management, Azure Functions, and service communication tools like Azure Service Bus.

The microservices pattern aligns perfectly with the goals of agility, scalability, and resilience in cloud-native development. However, implementing it requires careful planning around service boundaries, communication, data management, deployment, and monitoring.

Principles of the Microservices Pattern

At its core, the microservices architecture adheres to the following principles:

- **Single Responsibility**: Each microservice encapsulates a specific business function.

- **Independent Deployment**: Services can be developed, deployed, and scaled independently.

- **Decentralized Data Management**: Each service owns its own data and schema.

- **Technology Agnosticism**: Services can use different programming languages and frameworks.

- **Resilience and Fault Isolation**: Failure in one service should not cascade to others.

- **DevOps and Automation**: CI/CD pipelines are essential to manage the complexity of multiple services.

These principles help organizations achieve faster release cycles, improved scalability, and better alignment of development teams with business domains.

Microservices in Azure: Core Building Blocks

Azure provides a robust set of tools and services to support the microservices pattern:

Component	Azure Service
Container Orchestration	Azure Kubernetes Service (AKS), Container Apps
Stateless Compute	Azure App Service, Azure Functions
Service Communication	Azure Service Bus, Event Grid, API Management
API Gateway	Azure API Management
Data Persistence	Cosmos DB, Azure SQL, Table Storage
Secrets Management	Azure Key Vault
Monitoring and Telemetry	Application Insights, Azure Monitor
CI/CD Pipelines	Azure DevOps, GitHub Actions

These services are modular and composable, enabling architects to build tailored microservice solutions.

Defining Service Boundaries

Proper service boundary design is crucial. A common strategy is to model services around **business capabilities**, aligning with the principles of **Domain-Driven Design (DDD)**.

For example, in an e-commerce system, you might identify the following microservices:

- **Product Service**
- **Inventory Service**
- **Order Service**
- **Payment Service**
- **Notification Service**
- **User Profile Service**

Each of these services can be developed independently, scaled based on its workload, and maintained by a dedicated team.

Communication Between Microservices

Microservices typically communicate via **HTTP REST APIs**, **gRPC**, or **messaging systems**. Azure supports both synchronous and asynchronous communication patterns:

Synchronous (REST, gRPC):

- Managed via **Azure API Management** to handle routing, throttling, versioning, and security.
- Ideal for real-time operations like user registration or order lookup.

Asynchronous (Message Bus, Eventing):

- Managed via **Azure Service Bus**, **Event Grid**, or **Event Hubs**.
- Suitable for decoupling services, handling retries, and improving resilience.

Example: Publish/Subscribe with Azure Service Bus

```
az servicebus namespace create \
—resource-group MyResourceGroup \
—name MyBusNamespace \
—location eastus
az servicebus topic create \
—resource-group MyResourceGroup \
—namespace-name MyBusNamespace \
—name OrderEvents
az servicebus subscription create \
```

—resource-group MyResourceGroup \

—namespace-name MyBusNamespace \

—topic-name OrderEvents \

—name InventorySubscription

This allows services to publish events like "OrderCreated" and have other services react accordingly.

Stateless and Stateful Services

In microservices architecture, services are ideally **stateless**, meaning they do not retain session information. However, some services require stateful behavior—like shopping carts or payment workflows.

Azure provides several options:

- **Stateless**: Azure Functions, Container Apps
- **Stateful**: Durable Functions, Azure Cosmos DB for session persistence, Azure Service Fabric (advanced scenarios)

Data Management Strategies

Each microservice typically owns its own data to avoid tight coupling. This approach is called **polyglot persistence**—services choose the most suitable data store.

Common patterns include:

- **Database-per-Service**: Services use different database technologies.

- **Event Sourcing**: Changes are stored as a series of events.

- **Command Query Responsibility Segregation (CQRS)**: Separates write and read models.

Example: Cosmos DB for Order Service

```
az cosmosdb create \

—resource-group MyResourceGroup \

—name mycosmosdbaccount \

—kind MongoDB \

—locations regionName=eastus failoverPriority=0 isZoneRedundant=false
```

Each microservice can implement its own Cosmos DB collection or container for domain-specific data.

Microservices Deployment and CI/CD

Deploying microservices individually is essential for agility and rollback. Azure DevOps and GitHub Actions provide CI/CD pipelines that support:

- Build and push Docker images to Azure Container Registry (ACR)

- Deploy services to AKS or Azure Container Apps

- Manage secrets via Key Vault integration
- Run integration and performance tests per service

Sample GitHub Action Workflow for AKS

```
jobs:
deploy:
runs-on: ubuntu-latest
steps:
- uses: actions/checkout@v2
- name: Azure Login
uses: azure/login@v1
with:
creds: ${{ secrets.AZURE_CREDENTIALS }}
- name: Deploy to AKS
run: |
kubectl apply -f k8s/order-service.yaml
```

API Gateway Pattern

To avoid tight coupling between clients and internal services, a centralized API Gateway is used. **Azure API Management** enables:

- Routing to backend services
- Request/response transformation

- Rate limiting and throttling
- Authentication and key validation
- Analytics and logging

Benefits:

- Abstracts microservices from clients
- Improves security posture
- Simplifies onboarding of new clients

Monitoring and Observability

In microservices, centralized logging and tracing are essential due to the distributed nature of services. Azure provides:

- **Application Insights**: Request tracing, dependency tracking, performance metrics
- **Log Analytics**: Aggregation and querying of structured logs
- **Azure Monitor**: Platform-wide observability

KQL Sample: Latency by Service

```
requests
| summarize avg(duration) by cloud_RoleName, bin(timestamp, 5m)
```

| order by avg_duration desc

This helps detect latency issues across different services.

Challenges and Anti-Patterns

While microservices offer many advantages, they come with challenges:

Challenge	Mitigation
Service Sprawl	Use service registries and naming conventions
Complex Deployments	Use CI/CD pipelines and container orchestrators
Data Consistency	Use eventual consistency, sagas, and compensation
Debugging and Tracing	Implement distributed tracing and correlation IDs
Over-Engineering	Start small, evolve with business needs

Avoid these anti-patterns:

- **Shared Database**: Violates data ownership and independence.
- **Tightly Coupled APIs**: Makes versioning and scaling difficult.
- **Too Many Services Too Soon**: Start with modular monolith if needed.

Real-World Example: Retail Platform on Azure

A retail company builds a global commerce platform using microservices. The architecture includes:

- **Azure Kubernetes Service (AKS)** to host containerized services
- **Azure API Management** as the unified gateway
- **Azure Cosmos DB** and **Azure SQL** for data persistence
- **Azure Event Grid** for asynchronous event delivery
- **Azure DevOps** for CI/CD automation
- **Application Insights** for centralized monitoring

Services are structured by domain:

- **Catalog Service**: Manages product listings
- **Cart Service**: Handles user carts (stateful via Cosmos DB)
- **Checkout Service**: Orchestrates order placement
- **Shipping Service**: Integrated with logistics APIs

The platform supports blue-green deployments and auto-scales based on traffic.

Summary

The microservices pattern is a powerful model for building agile, scalable, and maintainable systems in Azure. By decomposing applications into autonomous services, organizations gain the flexibility to innovate, scale selectively, and respond quickly to market demands.

Key takeaways:

- Microservices align with cloud-native principles of independence and resilience.
- Azure offers a rich ecosystem—AKS, Container Apps, API Management, Cosmos DB, and DevOps tools—that support the entire lifecycle.
- Communication, data ownership, and observability are critical concerns.
- A successful microservices journey requires disciplined design, governance, and monitoring.

The next section will build upon this foundation by diving into CQRS (Command Query Responsibility Segregation), another key pattern for optimizing data handling in distributed systems.

The CQRS Pattern (Command Query Responsibility Segregation)

The Command Query Responsibility Segregation (CQRS) pattern is a powerful architectural approach that separates the responsibilities of reading data (queries) and modifying data (commands) into distinct models. This separation enables optimized, scalable, and maintainable applications, particularly when dealing with complex domains, high-performance requirements, or event-driven systems.

In Azure, CQRS can be effectively implemented using a combination of services such as **Azure Cosmos DB**, **Azure SQL Database**, **Azure Service Bus**, **Azure Functions**, and **Event Grid**. This section provides an in-depth exploration of CQRS, including its structure, implementation strategies, benefits, trade-offs, and real-world applications.

Core Concepts of CQRS

The CQRS pattern divides an application into two distinct paths:

- **Command Model**: Handles requests that change state (e.g., create, update, delete). These operations are processed via command handlers.
- **Query Model**: Handles requests that read data. This model is optimized for fast data retrieval, often denormalized for performance.

By decoupling reads from writes, CQRS promotes **separation of concerns**, **scalability**, and **specialization** of each model.

Comparison

Concern	Command Model	Query Model
Purpose	Modify data	Read data
Optimization	Consistency and integrity	Performance and flexibility
Storage	Normalized schema	Denormalized schema
Latency	Can be asynchronous	Typically synchronous

Benefits of CQRS

1. **Scalability**: Read and write workloads can be scaled independently.
2. **Performance**: Query model can be tailored for fast reads using caching and denormalization.
3. **Security**: Commands and queries can have different access controls and authorization paths.
4. **Flexibility**: Supports multiple read models for different client applications.
5. **Compatibility with Event Sourcing**: Naturally complements systems that use event logs for state management.

CQRS in Azure: Service Mapping

Azure provides a rich set of tools to build CQRS architectures:

Pattern Component	Azure Service
Command Handler	Azure Functions, Azure App Service
Message Bus	Azure Service Bus, Event Grid
Write Store	Azure SQL, Cosmos DB (OLTP)
Query Store	Cosmos DB, Azure Search, Redis, Synapse
API Layer	Azure API Management
Monitoring	Application Insights, Log Analytics

Implementing the Command Side

The **Command Side** processes incoming commands such as CreateOrder, UpdateUser, or DeleteInventoryItem. These commands may go through validation, authorization, and processing before writing to the database.

Commands should be handled asynchronously for scalability and responsiveness. Azure Functions with Service Bus triggers are ideal for this.

Example: Azure Function as a Command Handler

```
module.exports = async function (context, message) {

context.log('Processing command:', message);

const command = JSON.parse(message);

if (command.type === "CreateOrder") {

// Validate input

// Save to write database (Cosmos DB)

context.log(`Creating order for customer: ${command.customerId}`);
```

```
}

};
```

Commands are sent to the function via Service Bus:

```
az servicebus queue create \
—resource-group MyResourceGroup \
—namespace-name MyServiceBusNamespace \
—name CommandsQueue
```

Implementing the Query Side

The **Query Side** is optimized for retrieving data. It may use denormalized schemas, materialized views, or caching to enhance performance.

Azure Cosmos DB is particularly well-suited for this, offering:

- Low-latency reads
- Global distribution
- Flexible schemas
- SQL-like query language

In complex applications, the query model can be synchronized via background workers that subscribe to data change events.

Example: Denormalized Read Model

```
{
```

```
"orderId": "12345",
"customerName": "Alice",
"items": [
{ "product": "Laptop", "quantity": 1, "price": 1200 },
{ "product": "Mouse", "quantity": 2, "price": 25 }
],
"total": 1250,
"status": "Pending"
}
```

Such documents can be queried efficiently using:

```
SELECT c.orderId, c.customerName, c.total FROM c WHERE c.status = 'Pending'
```

Synchronizing Read and Write Models

CQRS introduces a challenge: ensuring the read model reflects changes from the write model. This is often handled through **event-driven synchronization.**

Azure Event Grid or Service Bus can publish events (e.g., OrderCreated, OrderShipped), and downstream services update the read model accordingly.

Example: Event Handler for Updating Read Model

```
module.exports = async function (context, eventGridEvent) {
```

```
const event = eventGridEvent.data;

if (event.eventType === 'OrderCreated') {

// Update read model (denormalized view)

context.log(`Updating read model for order ${event.orderId}`);

}

};
```

Events ensure **eventual consistency** between write and read models.

Eventual Consistency and Compensation

In a CQRS system, immediate consistency is not always guaranteed. Systems must tolerate **eventual consistency**—where the read model lags slightly behind the write.

To maintain business correctness, implement:

- **Compensation Logic**: Undo operations if something fails downstream
- **Idempotency**: Ensure processing the same message multiple times has no side effects
- **Correlation IDs**: Track requests across services

CQRS and Event Sourcing

CQRS is frequently paired with **Event Sourcing**, where changes to application state are stored as a sequence of events rather than overwriting data.

This model allows:

- Complete audit trails
- Rebuilding of state from event streams
- Easy integration with analytics pipelines

Azure Event Hubs or a Cosmos DB with a custom event schema can serve as the event store.

CI/CD Considerations

Each side of CQRS may have independent release cycles. Ensure:

- Isolated CI pipelines for command/query services
- Database migrations are backward-compatible
- Shared contracts (e.g., event schema) are versioned

Azure DevOps or GitHub Actions can be used to manage independent deployments and rollbacks.

Monitoring and Observability

Use **Application Insights** to trace requests across services. Implement structured logging with correlation IDs to track a command from initiation to read model update.

KQL Example: Trace a Command by Correlation ID

traces

| where customDimensions.CorrelationId == "abc-123"

| order by timestamp asc

Add alerts to detect excessive lag between write and read models.

Real-World Scenario: Banking Transactions

A banking platform uses CQRS to handle financial transactions:

- **Commands**: TransferFunds, Withdraw, Deposit—validated and processed by Azure Functions.
- **Write Store**: Azure SQL stores normalized, transactional records.
- **Events**: Published via Event Grid on transaction completion.
- **Query Store**: Cosmos DB holds account snapshots for fast dashboard queries.
- **Security**: RBAC restricts command execution to authorized users.
- **Monitoring**: Application Insights traces user actions and event propagation.

This separation of command and query paths enables robust auditing, responsive UIs, and scalable operations.

Summary

CQRS is a transformative pattern for applications with complex domains, high throughput, or strict scalability requirements. It enforces a clean separation between commands and queries, allowing each to evolve and scale independently.

Key takeaways:

- CQRS improves **performance**, **scalability**, and **domain clarity**.
- Azure provides first-class support through **Functions**, **Service Bus**, **Cosmos DB**, and **Event Grid**.
- Event-driven synchronization ensures **eventual consistency**.
- Proper **monitoring**, **idempotency**, and **contract versioning** are critical for production success.

The next section will build upon this by exploring Event Sourcing and Messaging—a natural extension of CQRS that unlocks advanced analytics, auditing, and rehydration capabilities.

Event Sourcing and Messaging

Event Sourcing and Messaging are core architectural patterns in modern distributed systems, especially those designed with domain-driven, microservices, or CQRS principles. Together, they enable highly decoupled, scalable, and resilient applications by treating events as first-class citizens and ensuring that every state change is recorded immutably.

In Azure, implementing these patterns is fully supported through services like **Azure Event Hubs**, **Azure Event Grid**, **Azure Service Bus**, and storage backends like **Cosmos DB**. These services work together to allow developers to build event-driven architectures (EDA), maintain detailed system audit trails, replay application state, and orchestrate complex workflows.

This section explains the structure, advantages, and implementation strategies of Event Sourcing and Messaging, offering practical guidance on how to design systems that are event-aware and durable.

What is Event Sourcing?

Event Sourcing is a pattern where state changes to an application are stored as a sequence of events. Instead of persisting the current state, the system records every change (event) that leads to the current state.

Example: Order Lifecycle

Instead of storing just the final order record:

- OrderCreated
- ItemAdded
- ShippingAddressUpdated
- OrderConfirmed
- OrderShipped

Each of these events is stored immutably and in sequence. The current state of the order can be reconstructed by **replaying** these events in order.

Benefits

- **Auditing**: Every state change is preserved and traceable.
- **Rehydration**: Reconstruct state at any point in time.

- **Debugging**: Time-travel debugging becomes possible.
- **Analytics**: Events can be used for reporting and anomaly detection.
- **Loose Coupling**: Write and read models can evolve independently.

Messaging Fundamentals

Messaging decouples the sender and receiver, enabling asynchronous, reliable, and scalable communication. There are two main messaging styles:

- **Point-to-point (Queue-based)**: A message is delivered to one consumer.
- **Publish-subscribe (Topic-based)**: A message is delivered to all subscribers.

In Azure, messaging is enabled through:

Service	Purpose
Service Bus	Enterprise-grade messaging, queues and topics
Event Grid	Lightweight, push-based event distribution
Event Hubs	High-throughput data ingestion

Azure Service Bus: Reliable Enterprise Messaging

Azure Service Bus is ideal for scenarios where message delivery guarantees and advanced messaging patterns are required.

Key Features

- FIFO with message sessions
- Duplicate detection
- Dead-letter queues
- Scheduled delivery
- Transactions and atomic sends/receives

Example: Creating a Topic and Subscriptions

az servicebus namespace create—resource-group MyRG—name mynamespace

az servicebus topic create—namespace-name mynamespace—name orders

az servicebus subscription create—namespace-name mynamespace—topic-name orders—name inventory

az servicebus subscription create—namespace-name mynamespace—topic-name orders—name notifications

With this, a single OrderCreated message is delivered to both the inventory and notifications services.

Azure Event Grid: Reactive Event Distribution

Event Grid is a fully managed event routing service that uses push-based delivery to send events to multiple handlers, such as Azure Functions, Logic Apps, or Event Hubs.

Features

- High-throughput, low-latency
- Built-in retry and dead-lettering
- Schema-based events (CloudEvents)
- Native integration with Azure resources

Example: Event Subscription for Blob Created

```
az eventgrid event-subscription create \
—name onBlobUpload \
—source-resource-id "/subscriptions/.../resourceGroups/.../providers/Microsoft.Storage/storageAccounts/mystorage" \
—endpoint-type azurefunction \
—endpoint "/subscriptions/.../resourceGroups/.../providers/Microsoft.Web/sites/myfunc/functions/ProcessBlob"
```

This reacts to Blob Storage events, triggering downstream logic.

Azure Event Hubs: Big Data Event Ingestion

Event Hubs is a high-throughput event ingestion service designed for telemetry, logging, and stream processing.

Use Cases

- Application telemetry

- IoT event streaming
- Clickstream and analytics pipelines

Architecture Highlights

- Event producers write into partitions.
- Event consumers (Stream Analytics, Functions, Databricks) read with checkpointing.
- Supports millions of events per second.

Event Hub Setup

az eventhubs namespace create—name myeventhubns—resource-group MyRG

az eventhubs eventhub create—name myeventhub—namespace-name myeventhubns—resource-group MyRG

Implementing Event Sourcing in Azure

Event sourcing in Azure often combines multiple services:

- Events are written to a store (e.g., Cosmos DB or Blob Storage)
- Events are emitted through Event Grid or Service Bus
- Downstream services process and project events into read models

Example Schema: Event Document in Cosmos DB


```
{
"id": "evt-123",
"aggregateId": "order-001",
"timestamp": "2025-04-01T14:23:00Z",
"eventType": "OrderCreated",
"payload": {
"orderId": "order-001",
"customerId": "cust-987",
"total": 149.99
}
}
```


Event documents are append-only and partitioned by aggregate ID for efficient replay.

Building Event Handlers

Azure Functions are commonly used as event handlers for both Event Grid and Service Bus.

Sample Event Grid Trigger

```
module.exports = async function (context, eventGridEvent) {
context.log(`Received event: ${eventGridEvent.eventType}`);
```

```
switch (eventGridEvent.eventType) {
case 'OrderCreated':
await updateReadModel(eventGridEvent.data);
break;
default:
context.log('Unknown event type');
}
};
```

Ensure idempotency by tracking processed event IDs.

Event Replay and Projections

To rebuild state or fix corrupted data, events can be replayed from the event store.

Strategies

- Use a consumer group checkpoint (in Event Hubs)
- Reprocess all events by timestamp
- Maintain read models via projections

Projections are views of data derived from one or more event types. These can be stored in Cosmos DB or cached in Redis for quick access.

Patterns Built on Events

Event Sourcing and Messaging support several architectural patterns:

- **Saga Pattern**: Manage long-running transactions via events and compensations.
- **Outbox Pattern**: Ensure messages are sent reliably after database changes.
- **Inbox Pattern**: Prevent duplicate event processing.
- **Change Data Capture (CDC)**: Emit events based on DB triggers or logs.

These patterns improve data consistency and system resilience.

Monitoring and Tracing Events

Event-driven systems must be observable to be reliable. Use:

- **Azure Monitor**: Tracks resource metrics
- **Application Insights**: Logs event processing times and errors
- **Diagnostic Logs**: For Event Grid, Service Bus, and Event Hubs
- **KQL Queries**: Analyze failures and retries

Example: Track Failed Event Deliveries

AzureDiagnostics

| where Category == "EventGridDiagnostics" and StatusCode != 200

| summarize count() by Resource, StatusCode, bin(TimeGenerated, 5m)

Set alerts to notify engineering teams of abnormal patterns.

Real-World Scenario: Logistics Tracking System

A logistics company builds a real-time tracking platform with:

- **Event Producers**: IoT devices emitting PackageScanned, PackageDispatched
- **Event Hubs**: Ingest high-volume telemetry
- **Azure Functions**: Process events, update statuses
- **Cosmos DB**: Store projections for fast lookup
- **Event Grid**: Notify customers and internal systems of state changes

This architecture is scalable, auditable, and reactive—able to handle millions of packages per day with end-to-end observability.

Summary

Event Sourcing and Messaging enable systems that are scalable, fault-tolerant, and audit-friendly. They shift the paradigm from storing state to storing a log of state-changing events, unlocking powerful patterns in modern cloud-native systems.

Key takeaways:

- Event Sourcing captures history, not just state.
- Messaging decouples components, enabling scalability and resilience.
- Azure provides robust tools: **Service Bus**, **Event Grid**, **Event Hubs**, and **Functions**.
- Replay, projections, and event-driven processing must be designed with idempotency and consistency in mind.
- Monitoring and diagnostics are essential in asynchronous architectures.

The next section will cover the API Gateway Pattern—how to present a unified entry point to your microservices and protect, route, and monitor access across the system.

API Gateway Pattern

The API Gateway pattern is a crucial architectural element in modern cloud-native systems, particularly those built using microservices or serverless paradigms. It acts as a single entry point for all client interactions with backend services, abstracting the complexities of service discovery, routing, versioning, and cross-cutting concerns like authentication, throttling, and logging.

In Azure, the API Gateway pattern is most commonly implemented using **Azure API Management (APIM)**. APIM offers a full suite of features that support RESTful APIs, OpenAPI specifications, transformation policies, analytics, monetization, and security. When properly implemented, an API Gateway improves system modularity, enhances developer experience, and centralizes governance.

This section explores the design principles, benefits, Azure implementations, and operational considerations of the API Gateway pattern, along with examples and real-world use cases.

Core Concepts of the API Gateway Pattern

At its essence, an API Gateway is a reverse proxy that:

- Accepts API calls from clients
- Routes them to the appropriate backend services
- Aggregates results (if needed)
- Applies policies like transformation, throttling, caching, and security
- Returns the response to the client

By sitting between clients and services, the API Gateway offers a centralized point for managing external access to internal systems.

Key Features

- Unified entry point
- Request/response transformation
- Authentication and authorization enforcement
- Rate limiting and quotas
- SSL termination
- Monitoring and analytics

Benefits of Using an API Gateway

1. **Decouples Clients and Services**: Clients don't need to know about service internals or endpoints.
2. **Security Centralization**: Implements consistent access controls and logging.
3. **Simplifies Mobile and Web Development**: Provides client-specific adaptations (e.g., response shaping).
4. **Eases Version Management**: Routes clients to correct versions of APIs.
5. **Improves Resilience**: Can integrate with retry, timeout, and circuit breaker policies.
6. **Supports Monetization**: Enable subscription plans, rate-limited access, and billing for third-party consumers.

Azure API Management (APIM)

Azure API Management is Microsoft's managed API gateway solution. It allows you to publish APIs to internal teams, external developers, and partners securely and at scale.

Components of APIM

- **API Gateway**: Routes and enforces policies
- **Publisher Portal**: Used by API publishers to manage APIs
- **Developer Portal**: Self-service portal for consuming APIs

- **Management Plane**: APIs and automation for lifecycle management

Deployment Options

- **Consumption Tier**: Serverless, autoscaling, low cost
- **Developer Tier**: Evaluation and testing
- **Basic/Standard/Premium Tiers**: Production workloads, with VNET support and SLAs

---

Creating an API in APIM

Step 1: Create an API Management Instance

```
az apim create \
—name MyApiGateway \
—resource-group MyResourceGroup \
—publisher-email admin@example.com \
—publisher-name "My Company" \
—sku-name Consumption
```

Step 2: Import API Definition

You can import APIs via OpenAPI, WSDL, or manually:

```
az apim api import \
```

—resource-group MyResourceGroup \

—service-name MyApiGateway \

—path orders \

—api-id orders-api \

—specification-format OpenApi \

—specification-path ./orders-openapi.json

Step 3: Add Backend Service

Configure the backend URL in the APIM policy or through the portal.

Defining Policies

Policies are XML-based configurations that execute at different stages (inbound, backend, outbound, on-error). They can:

- Rewrite URLs
- Modify headers
- Validate tokens
- Add CORS support
- Set caching

Example: Add CORS Header and Set Rate Limit

<inbound>

```
<base />

<set-header name="Access-Control-Allow-Origin" exists-action="override">

<value>*</value>

</set-header>

<rate-limit calls="10" renewal-period="60" />

</inbound>
```

This allows cross-origin requests and limits calls to 10 per minute.

Authentication and Authorization

Azure API Management integrates with:

- **OAuth 2.0 and OpenID Connect** for securing APIs using Azure AD or third-party identity providers.
- **Subscription Keys** for access control and throttling.
- **Client Certificates** for mutual TLS.
- **JWT Token Validation** to secure APIs at the gateway.

JWT Validation Policy

```
<validate-jwt header-name="Authorization" failed-validation-httpcode="401" require-scheme="Bearer">

<openid-config url="https://login.microsoftonline.com/{tenant-id}/v2.0/.well-known/openid-configuration" />
```

```
<required-claims>

<claim name="aud">

<value>api://my-api</value>

</claim>

</required-claims>

</validate-jwt>
```

This ensures only tokens issued to the correct audience are accepted.

Caching and Performance

APIM supports response caching for GET requests to reduce load on backends and improve performance.

Example: Enable Output Caching

```
<inbound>

<cache-lookup vary-by-developer="false" vary-by-developer-groups="false" />

</inbound>

<backend>

<base />

</backend>

<outbound>

<cache-store duration="300" />
```

</outbound>

Monitoring and Analytics

APIM logs all request and response data, which can be exported to:

- **Azure Monitor**
- **Application Insights**
- **Log Analytics**
- **Event Hubs**

KQL Example: Identify High-Latency APIs

```
AzureDiagnostics
| where ResourceType == "APIManagementGateways"
| summarize avg(DurationMs) by ApiName_s
| order by avg_DurationMs desc
```

Use dashboards to track usage, errors, and consumer behaviors.

Versioning and Revisions

APIM supports:

- **Versions**: For breaking changes (v1, v2)
- **Revisions**: For backward-compatible edits

Clients can specify which version to use via:

- Path parameter: /v1/orders
- Header: api-version: v1
- Query string: ?api-version=v1

Versioning allows safe evolution of APIs while maintaining support for existing consumers.

Real-World Scenario: Multi-Channel E-Commerce Gateway

A global e-commerce platform implements an API Gateway using Azure APIM:

- Mobile apps, web clients, and third-party partners access the same unified gateway.
- **Mobile** clients receive compressed JSON.
- **Web** clients receive full HTML-rendered content.
- **Partners** are rate-limited and authenticated via client credentials.
- Internal services like Orders, Products, and Payments are routed securely via APIM policies.
- Developer portal allows onboarding and documentation for external teams.

The result is a simplified interface for consumers and a powerful governance layer for backend APIs.

Summary

The API Gateway pattern provides a robust mechanism for unifying access to diverse backend services, enabling centralized control, security, and visibility.

Key takeaways:

- Azure API Management is a complete platform for implementing the API Gateway pattern.
- Policies offer unmatched flexibility in shaping traffic and enforcing governance.
- Integrated security supports enterprise-grade authentication and access control.
- Versioning, caching, analytics, and monitoring are built-in and easy to configure.
- A well-designed gateway enhances developer productivity, system resilience, and scalability.

The next section will explore the **Strangler Fig Pattern and Anti-Corruption Layer**, essential strategies for safely modernizing legacy systems and integrating disparate architectures within Azure.

Strangler Fig and Anti-Corruption Layer

Modernizing legacy systems can be one of the most complex and risk-prone efforts in software development. However, with the right architectural patterns, you can evolve legacy applications safely, incrementally, and with minimal disruption. Two key patterns that support this transformation are the **Strangler Fig Pattern** and the **Anti-Corruption Layer (ACL)**.

In the Azure ecosystem, these patterns are not only feasible—they're practical and powerful, thanks to services like **Azure API Management**, **Azure Functions**, **Azure Logic Apps**, **Azure Service Bus**, and **Azure Kubernetes Service (AKS)**. This section explores how these patterns work, when to use them, and how to implement them effectively in Azure.

The Strangler Fig Pattern

Inspired by the strangler fig tree, which slowly envelops and replaces its host tree, the Strangler Fig Pattern involves gradually replacing parts of a legacy system by building new features around it, eventually strangling the old system entirely.

Characteristics

- **Incremental Migration**: New functionality is built as independent services.
- **Parallel Operation**: Old and new systems coexist temporarily.
- **Facade Routing**: A routing layer determines whether to send a request to the legacy or modern component.
- **Low Risk**: Allows testing and validation without big-bang rewrites.

Benefits

- Reduces risk of large-scale refactoring failures
- Enables faster delivery of new features

- Preserves business continuity
- Supports microservices adoption

Implementing the Strangler Fig in Azure

A typical implementation involves setting up an **API Gateway**, using it to direct requests to either the legacy system or the new microservices.

Step 1: Place an API Gateway in Front

Use **Azure API Management** to expose all APIs—legacy and modern—from a unified gateway.

```
az apim api import \
—resource-group MyResourceGroup \
—service-name MyApiGateway \
—path orders \
—api-id legacy-orders \
—specification-format OpenApi \
—specification-path ./legacy-orders-openapi.json
```

Step 2: Route Requests Conditionally

Use policies to route to different backends based on the path or headers.

```
<inbound>
```

```
<choose>

<when
condition="@(context.Request.OriginalUrl.Path.Contains(&quot;/v2/

<set-backend-service base-url="https://new-api.azurewebsites.net"
/>

</when>

<otherwise>

<set-backend-service base-url="https://legacy-api.company.com" />

</otherwise>

</choose>

</inbound>
```

Example: Modernizing Order Processing

Let's say a legacy monolith handles order processing, but the business wants to introduce new capabilities like real-time inventory validation.

1. **Wrap the legacy endpoint** in APIM.
2. **Build a new service** (e.g., Azure Function) that handles inventory logic.
3. **Introduce feature toggles** or headers that determine which version to use.
4. **Slowly route traffic** from /orders/v1 to /orders/v2.
5. **Retire the old endpoint** once 100% of traffic has shifted.

Monitoring the Transition

Use **Azure Monitor** and **Application Insights** to:

- Track traffic patterns
- Identify errors
- Measure latency differences between old and new systems

```
requests
| where url contains "/orders"
| summarize count() by name, url, bin(timestamp, 5m)
```

This helps validate the behavior and adoption of the new implementation before turning off the old one.

The Anti-Corruption Layer (ACL)

The Anti-Corruption Layer pattern provides a protective boundary between the legacy system and the new system. It ensures the new system doesn't inherit the poor design, inconsistencies, or technical debt of the legacy codebase.

ACL Responsibilities

- Translates models and protocols between systems
- Ensures encapsulation and boundary protection
- Allows new systems to evolve independently
- Prevents data leaks or coupling

Implementing ACL in Azure

ACLs can be implemented using intermediate services or logic layers that normalize interactions.

Common Components

- **Azure Functions**: Implement transformation logic as lightweight services.
- **Azure Logic Apps**: For orchestrating calls across disparate systems.
- **Azure Service Bus**: For messaging-based integration with retry and dead-lettering.
- **Azure API Management**: For facade interfaces and protocol bridging.

Example: Using Azure Function as ACL

```
module.exports = async function (context, req) {

const legacyRequest = transformToLegacyFormat(req.body);

const response = await callLegacySystem(legacyRequest);

const normalizedResponse = transformFromLegacyFormat(response);

context.res = {

status: 200,

body: normalizedResponse
```

};

};

This approach prevents legacy-specific logic or naming from leaking into the new architecture.

Data Mapping and Transformation

One of the hardest parts of an ACL is mapping data models. Common tools and techniques include:

- **JSON Schema Mapping**
- **Model-to-Model Transformers**
- **Adapter Design Pattern**
- **Automated Data Mapping Tools** (e.g., Azure Data Factory for bulk mappings)

Example: Logic App Transform

In Azure Logic Apps, you can use a **Data Operations – Compose** action with expressions to reformat legacy output before passing it to a new service.

```
{
"fullName": "@concat(triggerOutputs()?['firstName'], ' ', triggerOutputs()?['lastName'])",
"email": "@triggerOutputs()?['emailAddress']"
}
```

Managing Complexity

Use **bounded contexts** to isolate legacy from modern code. Each system owns its domain logic and interacts through well-defined contracts.

- Introduce **shared contracts** via OpenAPI specs
- Document **translation rules**
- Store **intermediate schemas** in version control
- Apply **versioning** rigorously to avoid breaking changes

Real-World Scenario: ERP Modernization

A manufacturing company modernizes its ERP:

- Legacy SAP exposes SOAP services
- APIM converts SOAP to REST via transformation policies
- ACL implemented using Azure Functions normalizes data
- Orders are routed to the legacy system unless marked as modern:true
- Over 6 months, new services (e.g., invoicing, shipping) are carved out and exposed via /v2

This phased approach enables modernization with minimal risk, full observability, and iterative value delivery.

Summary

The Strangler Fig and Anti-Corruption Layer patterns are vital strategies for evolving legacy systems without risking downtime or instability. Together, they support clean modernization by enabling new services to coexist with and eventually replace old ones.

Key takeaways:

- The **Strangler Fig Pattern** allows for incremental migration, reducing risk.
- The **API Gateway** enables facade-based routing and feature toggling.
- The **Anti-Corruption Layer** ensures clean boundaries between legacy and modern systems.
- Azure provides robust tooling—**APIM**, **Functions**, **Logic Apps**, **Service Bus**—for implementing these patterns.
- Proper monitoring, versioning, and data transformation are critical for success.

These patterns pave the way for a controlled and effective transition from legacy to cloud-native systems, setting the foundation for more resilient, maintainable, and agile architectures. The next chapter focuses on high-performance patterns for optimizing system responsiveness and throughput.

Chapter 5: High-Performance Patterns

Caching Strategies with Azure Redis Cache

Caching is one of the most effective techniques for improving application performance and reducing latency. It enables data to be stored in a high-speed, in-memory location so that future requests for that data can be served faster. In cloud-native architectures, where speed and scalability are crucial, implementing caching strategies appropriately can dramatically improve user experience and reduce infrastructure costs.

Azure provides a fully managed caching service in the form of **Azure Cache for Redis**, which supports various caching patterns and is compatible with open-source Redis. This section explores caching principles, strategies, patterns, and best practices in the context of Azure, focusing on how to design scalable and performant applications using Azure Redis Cache.

Why Caching Matters

In distributed systems and microservice-based architectures, services often depend on frequent access to data, configuration, and computation results. Without caching, each request might:

- Query a database
- Call an external API
- Perform expensive computations

This increases response time, degrades performance under load, and raises operational costs. Caching mitigates these issues by reducing the round trips to backends and delivering data directly from memory.

Azure Cache for Redis Overview

Azure Cache for Redis is a fully managed in-memory data store built on the popular open-source Redis. It offers low-latency, high-throughput capabilities and is suitable for use as:

- A data cache
- A session store
- A message broker
- A pub/sub event system

Key Features

- Sub-millisecond latency
- Persistent backups (Premium tier)
- Geo-replication and clustering
- Active-active cache with Redis Enterprise
- TLS encryption and VNet support

Provisioning Azure Cache for Redis

az redis create \

—name myCache \

—resource-group myResourceGroup \

—location eastus \

—sku Basic \

—vm-size C1

This command provisions a basic Redis cache. For production scenarios, use **Standard** or **Premium** tiers for high availability and performance features.

Caching Strategies and Patterns

There are several common caching strategies, each with its own advantages and trade-offs.

1. Cache Aside (Lazy Loading)

In this pattern, the application checks the cache before querying the database.

Workflow:

1. Try to get data from cache
2. If a cache miss, query the database
3. Update cache with the new data

```
const key = `user:${userId}`;

let user = await redis.get(key);

if (!user) {

user = await db.queryUserById(userId);
```

```
await redis.set(key, JSON.stringify(user), 'EX', 3600); // Set TTL
}
```

Pros:

- Only caches what's needed
- Prevents stale data on writes

Cons:

- First request is slow
- Potential cache stampede if many requests miss at once

---

2. Write-Through Cache

In this strategy, data is written to the cache and database at the same time.

```
await db.saveUser(user);
await redis.set(`user:${user.id}`, JSON.stringify(user));
```

Pros:

- Cache is always populated
- Fast reads for all future requests

Cons:

- Write latency is higher
- Complex error handling on write failure

---

3. Read-Through Cache

A layer between the application and cache handles all reads, loading data from the database on cache misses automatically.

Used commonly in middleware or repository classes.

Pros:

- Transparent to business logic
- Ensures centralized caching policy

Cons:

- Complexity increases
- Requires integration in data access layer

---

4. Refresh-Ahead

Proactively refreshes cache entries before they expire.

Use Case: Time-sensitive data that is frequently accessed.

```
// Background job runs every 10 minutes

const user = await db.queryUserById(userId);

await redis.set(`user:${userId}`, JSON.stringify(user), 'EX', 3600);
```

Pros:

- Reduced chance of cache misses

- Better control over expiration behavior

Cons:

- May refresh unused data
- Higher background compute cost

Advanced Caching Patterns

1. Distributed Sessions

Use Redis to store user session state in stateless applications (e.g., on App Service or AKS).

```
dotnet add package Microsoft.Extensions.Caching.StackExchangeRedis

services.AddSession();

services.AddStackExchangeRedisCache(options =>

{

options.Configuration = Configuration["Redis:ConnectionString"];

});
```

2. Full Page or Fragment Caching

Cache rendered HTML responses or UI fragments for static or semi-static content.

- Suitable for marketing pages or product catalogs

- Can be implemented with API Gateway or CDN layer + Redis backend

3. Rate Limiting

Use Redis as a counter store to rate-limit users or API consumers.

```
const key = `rate-limit:${userId}`;

let count = await redis.incr(key);

if (count === 1) {

await redis.expire(key, 60); // 1-minute window

}

if (count > 100) {

throw new Error('Rate limit exceeded');

}
```

Data Expiry and Eviction

Redis supports Time-To-Live (TTL) on keys and multiple eviction policies:

- **noeviction**: Returns an error when memory is full
- **volatile-lru**: Evicts least recently used keys with TTL
- **allkeys-lru**: Evicts LRU from all keys
- **volatile-ttl**: Evicts keys with shortest TTL
- **allkeys-random**: Random eviction

Choose eviction policies based on use case and memory constraints.

Monitoring and Scaling Redis in Azure

Use **Azure Monitor** and **Redis Metrics** to track:

- Memory usage
- CPU load
- Cache hit ratio
- Connection count
- Operations/sec

Example: Set an Alert for High CPU Usage

```
az monitor metrics alert create \
—name RedisHighCPU \
—resource-group myResourceGroup \
—scopes /subscriptions/{id}/resourceGroups/myResourceGroup/providers/Microsoft.Cache/Redis/myCache \
—condition "avg percentageCpu > 80" \
—description "High CPU Alert for Redis"
```

Security and Best Practices

- Use **SSL** to encrypt Redis connections

- Deploy within **Virtual Network (VNet)** for private access
- Use **firewall rules** and **Azure AD-based RBAC**
- Avoid storing sensitive data like passwords in Redis
- Apply **data encryption at rest and in transit**

Real-World Scenario: E-Commerce Website

A global retailer uses Azure Redis Cache for:

- **Product catalog**: Cached via Cache-Aside for read-heavy performance
- **User sessions**: Managed via Distributed Cache for App Service
- **Shopping carts**: Stored temporarily in Redis with TTL
- **Flash sales**: Rate-limited per user via Redis counters
- **Recommendation engine**: Cached results of ML predictions

This architecture delivers sub-100ms responses during peak events like Black Friday, while ensuring cost control and elasticity.

Summary

Caching is a foundational pattern for achieving low latency and high throughput in distributed cloud applications. With Azure Cache for Redis, you can implement a variety of strategies—from simple key-value caching to complex session and rate-limiting logic.

Key takeaways:

- Choose the right caching strategy based on read/write patterns and data volatility.
- Azure Redis Cache offers low-latency, scalable caching with multiple deployment tiers.
- Use TTLs, eviction policies, and refresh mechanisms to manage cache memory efficiently.
- Monitor cache performance and scale proactively to meet demand.
- Secure your Redis instances with encryption, VNet integration, and access policies.

In the next section, we'll examine asynchronous messaging with Azure Service Bus—a critical component for decoupling systems and enabling reliable, distributed workflows.

Asynchronous Messaging with Azure Service Bus

Asynchronous messaging is a cornerstone of distributed system design. It decouples communication between services, improves scalability, enables resiliency in the face of transient failures, and facilitates complex workflows. In Azure, asynchronous messaging is supported primarily through **Azure Service Bus**, a fully managed enterprise messaging service built for high availability, durability, and integration with Azure's broader ecosystem.

This section explores asynchronous messaging principles and strategies using Azure Service Bus. We'll cover architecture, use cases, message delivery models, integration patterns, advanced features, security, and monitoring. By the end, you'll understand how to implement reliable, scalable, and maintainable messaging solutions in Azure.

Why Asynchronous Messaging?

In synchronous communication (e.g., REST APIs), services wait for responses, creating tight coupling and latency bottlenecks. Asynchronous messaging offers key benefits:

- **Loose coupling**: Producers and consumers operate independently.
- **Load leveling**: Consumers process messages at their own pace.
- **Resilience**: Retry mechanisms mitigate transient errors.
- **Scalability**: Message queues buffer bursts of traffic.
- **Event-driven architecture**: Enables real-time data flows and reactive systems.

Azure Service Bus Overview

Azure Service Bus is designed for enterprise-grade messaging, supporting **message queues** and **publish/subscribe** patterns.

Key Concepts

Concept	Description
Queue	First-in-first-out (FIFO) delivery to one consumer
Topic + Subscription	Pub/sub model for multiple consumers
Session	Enables ordered, stateful message processing
Dead-letter Queue	Stores undeliverable or rejected messages

Tiers

- **Basic**: Queues only, no advanced features
- **Standard**: Queues + topics, duplicate detection, sessions
- **Premium**: Dedicated resources, high throughput, VNet support

---

Provisioning Azure Service Bus

az servicebus namespace create \

—resource-group MyResourceGroup \

—name myServiceBusNamespace \

—location eastus \

—sku Standard

az servicebus queue create \

```
—namespace-name myServiceBusNamespace \
—name orders-queue \
—resource-group MyResourceGroup
```

Messaging Patterns

1. Point-to-Point (Queue)

- Producer sends a message to a queue
- A single consumer processes each message

```
await sender.sendMessages({
body: { orderId: '123', items: [...] },
messageId: 'order-123'
});
```

Use this for task distribution, background processing, or job queues.

2. Publish-Subscribe (Topic + Subscription)

- Producer sends a message to a topic
- Multiple subscriptions receive the message independently

```
az servicebus topic create \
—name new-orders \
—namespace-name myServiceBusNamespace
```

az servicebus subscription create \

—topic-name new-orders \

—name billing-subscription \

—namespace-name myServiceBusNamespace

Used for events like OrderCreated, where billing, shipping, and notifications all respond independently.

Advanced Features

Message Sessions

Used to enforce **FIFO** processing with affinity across a series of related messages (e.g., per customer or order).

const receiver = serviceBusClient.acceptSession("orders-queue", "session-id");

const message = await receiver.receiveMessages(1);

Dead-Letter Queues (DLQ)

Messages that can't be delivered (e.g., after max retries) are moved to the DLQ.

Reasons:

- Expired TTL
- Too many delivery attempts
- Message rejected by receiver

az servicebus queue create—name myqueue—enable-dead-lettering-on-message-expiration true

Consume DLQ messages for diagnostics or retries.

Integration Patterns

Command Messaging

Use queues to submit commands (e.g., ShipOrder), processed by a single service.

Event Notification

Use topics to publish events (e.g., ProductBackInStock), consumed by many services.

Deferred Processing

Schedule messages to be delivered in the future (delayed delivery).

await sender.scheduleMessages(message, scheduledEnqueueTime);

Correlation IDs

Include a correlation ID for distributed tracing:

await sender.sendMessages({

body: payload,

applicationProperties: {

correlationId: "req-456"

```
}
});
```

Reliability and Exactly-Once Processing

Azure Service Bus supports **at least once** delivery. To implement **idempotency**:

- Use message IDs and deduplication
- Store processed message IDs
- Design consumers to handle duplicate messages gracefully

Enable duplicate detection:

```
az servicebus queue create \
—name dedup-queue \
—namespace-name myServiceBusNamespace \
—duplicate-detection-history-time-window PT10M
```

Monitoring and Troubleshooting

Use **Azure Monitor**, **Log Analytics**, and **Application Insights** for:

- Message throughput
- Queue length and active message count
- Dead-letter messages
- Failed deliveries

KQL Example: Queue Message Count

```
AzureMetrics

| where Resource == "orders-queue"

| where MetricName == "ActiveMessages"

| summarize avg(Total) by bin(TimeGenerated, 5m)
```

Set alerts on thresholds (e.g., >10,000 messages pending) to detect processing delays.

Scaling Consumers

Azure Functions, WebJobs, AKS pods, or VMs can process messages from Service Bus.

- Use **Concurrency control** to match processing capacity
- Enable **batch processing** to reduce network overhead
- Apply **retry policies** and **circuit breakers** for resilience

Example: Azure Function with Service Bus Trigger

```
[FunctionName("ProcessOrder")]

public void Run(

[ServiceBusTrigger("orders-queue", Connection = "ServiceBusConnection")] string myQueueItem,

ILogger log)
```

```
{
log.LogInformation($"Processing order: {myQueueItem}");
}
```

Security and Access Control

- **Shared Access Policies**: Grant scoped rights (e.g., send, listen)
- **Managed Identities**: Secure access without credentials
- **Virtual Network**: Restrict access to private resources (Premium tier)
- **Firewall Rules**: Limit IP-based access

Assigning Send Permission to a Managed Identity

```
az role assignment create \
—assignee <principalId> \
—role "Azure Service Bus Data Sender" \
—scope "/subscriptions/{subId}/resourceGroups/{rg}/providers/Microsoft.ServiceBus/namespaces/{ns}"
```

Real-World Scenario: Online Grocery Platform

A grocery delivery app implements asynchronous workflows with Service Bus:

- **Checkout Service** sends OrderPlaced to a topic

- **Inventory Service** subscribes to check stock and update availability
- **Billing Service** initiates payment and emits PaymentProcessed
- **Logistics Service** schedules delivery via delayed messages
- **Notification Service** sends confirmations to users

Dead-letter queues capture processing failures and are monitored via Application Insights. The platform handles millions of daily transactions with elasticity, resilience, and traceability.

Summary

Asynchronous messaging with Azure Service Bus enables scalable, decoupled, and resilient application architectures. Whether you're building microservices, event-driven systems, or background job pipelines, Service Bus offers enterprise-level reliability and advanced capabilities.

Key takeaways:

- Use queues for command dispatching and tasks
- Use topics and subscriptions for event-driven fan-out
- Implement dead-letter queues and retry logic for fault tolerance
- Integrate with Azure Functions for serverless processing

- Secure messaging endpoints with RBAC and managed identities

- Monitor system health and queue depth to maintain throughput

In the next section, we'll explore how to leverage Azure Batch and Durable Functions for parallel processing and large-scale background workloads.

Parallel Processing with Azure Batch and Durable Functions

Parallel processing is essential for modern cloud applications that handle large datasets, computationally intensive operations, or concurrent workflows. Whether you're transcoding video files, analyzing telemetry data, or orchestrating microservices, Azure provides robust services to design scalable, efficient, and fault-tolerant parallel processing pipelines.

Azure offers two primary solutions for parallel workloads:

- **Azure Batch**: A platform for large-scale parallel and high-performance computing (HPC).

- **Azure Durable Functions**: An extension of Azure Functions that enables stateful, serverless workflows including fan-out/fan-in patterns.

This section explores both services in depth, comparing their strengths, typical use cases, and integration patterns. We'll walk through real-world scenarios and provide design guidance to help you build parallel processing solutions that are secure, maintainable, and cost-efficient.

Understanding Parallel Processing

Parallel processing refers to dividing a task into subtasks that can be executed simultaneously, leveraging multiple processors or threads. This reduces total execution time, improves resource utilization, and enables horizontal scaling.

Key Concepts

- **Task Decomposition**: Breaking work into independent units
- **Concurrency**: Executing multiple tasks simultaneously
- **Fan-Out/Fan-In**: Dispatching tasks in parallel and aggregating results
- **State Management**: Tracking task progress and outcomes
- **Fault Tolerance**: Retrying or rerouting failed tasks

Azure Batch Overview

Azure Batch is a cloud-scale job scheduling and compute management platform. It enables you to run parallel tasks across a pool of virtual machines without manually provisioning infrastructure.

Key Features

- Automatic VM scaling and pool management

- Support for Windows and Linux workloads
- Integration with custom scripts, Docker containers, and apps
- Flexible job/task dependency graphs
- Persistent output to Blob Storage

Common Use Cases

- Video rendering and transcoding
- Scientific simulations and modeling
- Monte Carlo and risk simulations
- Data preprocessing and ETL pipelines
- Image and document processing

Getting Started with Azure Batch

Step 1: Create a Batch Account

az batch account create \

—name mybatchaccount \

—resource-group myresourcegroup \

—location eastus \

—storage-account mystorageaccount

Step 2: Create a Compute Pool

```
az batch pool create \
—id mypool \
—vm-size Standard_D2_v2 \
—target-dedicated-nodes 5 \
—image canonical:ubuntuserver:18.04-LTS:latest \
—node-agent-sku-id "batch.node.ubuntu 18.04"
```

Step 3: Add Jobs and Tasks

```
az batch job create—id myjob—pool-id mypool
az batch task create \
—job-id myjob \
—task-id task1 \
—command-line "/bin/bash -c 'python process_data.py'"
```

Tasks run in parallel across available nodes in the pool.

Azure Durable Functions Overview

Durable Functions are an extension of Azure Functions that allow you to write stateful workflows in a serverless environment. They support the **fan-out/fan-in** pattern to execute multiple functions in parallel and wait for their completion.

Key Features

- Orchestrator functions for workflow coordination
- Activity functions for individual units of work
- Durable timers and checkpoints
- Built-in retry and state management
- No need to manage infrastructure

Common Use Cases

- Batch file processing
- Long-running data pipelines
- Microservice orchestration
- Event-driven chaining of tasks

Implementing Fan-Out/Fan-In with Durable Functions

Step 1: Define Activity Function

```
[FunctionName("ProcessFile")]

public static async Task<string> RunActivity(

[ActivityTrigger] string fileName,

ILogger log)
```

```
{
log.LogInformation($"Processing file: {fileName}");
// Simulate work
await Task.Delay(2000);
return $"{fileName} processed";
}
```

Step 2: Define Orchestrator Function

```
[FunctionName("Orchestrator")]
public static async Task<List<string>> RunOrchestrator(
[OrchestrationTrigger] IDurableOrchestrationContext context)
{
var files = context.GetInput<List<string>>();
var tasks = new List<Task<string>>();
foreach (var file in files)
{
tasks.Add(context.CallActivityAsync<string>("ProcessFile", file));
}
await Task.WhenAll(tasks);
return tasks.Select(t => t.Result).ToList();
}
```

Step 3: Start the Workflow

```
[FunctionName("StartProcessing")]

public static async Task<HttpResponseMessage> Start(

[HttpTrigger(AuthorizationLevel.Function, "post")] HttpRequestMessage req,

[DurableClient] IDurableOrchestrationClient starter)

{

var files = await req.Content.ReadAsAsync<List<string>>();

string instanceId = await starter.StartNewAsync("Orchestrator", files);

return starter.CreateCheckStatusResponse(req, instanceId);

}
```

Choosing Between Azure Batch and Durable Functions

Criteria	Azure Batch	Azure Durable Functions
Workload Type	HPC, batch jobs, VM-level tasks	Serverless orchestration, micro-tasks
Infrastructure Control	Full control of VMs, containers	Abstracted, managed by Azure
Scale	Massive, across hundreds of VMs	Good for lightweight, parallel functions
Task Duration	Minutes to hours	Seconds to minutes
Data Volume	Large files, datasets	JSON or small payloads
Billing Model	Based on VM usage	Per execution and resource consumption

Use **Batch** when you need compute-intensive processing. Use **Durable Functions** for event-driven coordination of tasks or microservices.

Parallel Processing Design Considerations

- **Idempotency**: Ensure that retrying a task doesn't corrupt data.
- **Timeouts and Retries**: Configure retry policies for transient failures.
- **Throttling**: Avoid overwhelming backends by controlling concurrency.
- **Task Granularity**: Balance between task size and scheduling overhead.

- **State Storage**: Durable Functions automatically manage state; Azure Batch requires external state tracking.
- **Monitoring**: Track task statuses, errors, and duration for visibility and optimization.

Monitoring and Diagnostics

Azure Batch

- View job/task statuses via the portal or CLI
- Export logs to Azure Storage
- Enable VM diagnostics for troubleshooting

```
az batch task show—job-id myjob—task-id task1
```

Durable Functions

- Use **Application Insights** for orchestration tracing
- Track custom metrics and function logs
- Enable durable function diagnostics

```
customEvents
| where name == "FunctionCompleted"
| summarize count() by tostring(customDimensions.FunctionName)
```

Real-World Scenario: Insurance Document Processing

An insurance company processes thousands of claims daily.

- **Azure Durable Functions** orchestrate intake workflows:
  - OCR extraction from scanned forms
  - Fraud detection checks
  - Notification emails to clients
- **Azure Batch** is used for:
  - Image preprocessing
  - Large-scale document classification via ML models
  - Archival to cold storage

The hybrid architecture provides elasticity, cost control, and fine-grained failure recovery.

Summary

Parallel processing unlocks the ability to handle demanding workloads with speed and efficiency. Whether you're processing big data, orchestrating microservices, or managing workflows, Azure Batch and Durable Functions provide scalable solutions tailored to your needs.

Key takeaways:

- **Azure Batch** is best for compute-intensive, long-running parallel jobs.
- **Durable Functions** excel in orchestrating short, stateful workflows serverlessly.
- Use fan-out/fan-in patterns to maximize concurrency and minimize execution time.
- Monitor, retry, and ensure idempotency to maintain reliability at scale.
- Azure provides seamless tooling to manage, track, and secure your parallel workloads.

With high-performance patterns like these in place, your applications are prepared to handle large-scale demand efficiently. The next chapter will focus on Security Patterns in Azure to ensure your systems remain protected, compliant, and resilient against threats.

Chapter 6: Security Patterns in Azure

Perimeter Security and Network Segmentation

In cloud-native architecture, security must be embedded at every layer. While traditional data centers relied heavily on a strong perimeter (e.g., firewalls and DMZs), Azure encourages a more **zero-trust, defense-in-depth** approach. That said, securing the perimeter remains a foundational aspect—especially when integrating hybrid environments, exposing APIs to external users, or protecting sensitive workloads.

In Azure, perimeter security is reinforced through **Network Security Groups (NSGs)**, **Azure Firewall**, **Azure DDoS Protection**, **Application Gateway with Web Application Firewall (WAF)**, and **Private Endpoints**. When coupled with **network segmentation**, organizations can isolate workloads, enforce least privilege, and reduce the blast radius of potential breaches.

This section will explore best practices and strategies for establishing strong perimeter defenses and designing secure, segmented network topologies in Azure.

Key Principles of Network Security

- **Zero Trust Networking**: Never trust, always verify—assume breach and enforce least privilege across all layers.
- **Micro-Segmentation**: Isolate workloads by function, sensitivity, and environment (e.g., Dev/Test/Prod).

- **Defense in Depth**: Layered security including firewalls, WAFs, DDoS protection, and identity controls.

- **East-West vs. North-South Traffic**: Secure internal (east-west) traffic as much as ingress/egress (north-south).

- **Log and Monitor Everything**: All network access and security events should be logged and reviewed.

Azure Virtual Network (VNet) Segmentation

A **Virtual Network (VNet)** in Azure is the foundation of private network isolation. Within a VNet, **subnets** segment traffic, and **NSGs** control flow at the subnet or NIC level.

Subnet Segmentation Example

- **Subnet-Web**: Hosts public-facing services (e.g., App Service with VNet Integration)

- **Subnet-App**: Internal APIs and services

- **Subnet-DB**: Private database servers (e.g., Azure SQL with Private Endpoint)

- **Subnet-Bastion**: Secure jump hosts (Azure Bastion)

Each subnet has its own NSG to control access in and out.

az network nsg rule create \

—resource-group MyRG \

—nsg-name WebSubnetNSG \

```
—name AllowHTTP \
—priority 100 \
—direction Inbound \
—access Allow \
—protocol Tcp \
—source-address-prefix Internet \
—destination-port-ranges 80
```

Network Security Groups (NSGs)

NSGs provide stateful packet filtering for both inbound and outbound traffic. Use NSGs to:

- Allow/deny access by IP address, port, protocol
- Apply rules to subnets or individual NICs
- Log and monitor traffic via NSG flow logs

Best Practices:

- Deny by default; explicitly allow necessary ports
- Apply NSGs at the subnet level for broad control
- Use service tags (e.g., AzureLoadBalancer, Internet, VirtualNetwork)
- Monitor NSG effectiveness with **Azure Network Watcher**

Azure Firewall

Azure Firewall is a fully stateful, managed firewall that scales dynamically and provides centralized policy control.

Features:

- Threat intelligence-based filtering (deny known bad IPs/domains)
- Application rules (FQDN filtering for HTTP/S)
- Network rules (protocol/port-based)
- Support for NAT and DNAT
- Integration with Azure Sentinel and Log Analytics

Deployment Pattern:

- Place Firewall in a **Hub VNet**
- Connect spoke VNets via VNet Peering or Virtual WAN
- Route traffic through the firewall using **User Defined Routes (UDRs)**

az network route-table route create \

—resource-group MyRG \

—route-table-name AppRouteTable \

—name RouteToFirewall \

—address-prefix 0.0.0.0/0 \

—next-hop-type VirtualAppliance \

—next-hop-ip-address 10.0.0.4

Application Gateway and Web Application Firewall (WAF)

Azure Application Gateway operates at Layer 7, offering advanced routing and security features.

WAF Capabilities:

- OWASP core rule sets
- SQL injection and XSS protection
- Bot mitigation
- Custom rules (e.g., block specific User-Agent headers)

Use WAF in **prevention mode** for production:

az network application-gateway waf-policy create \

—resource-group MyRG \

—name WAFPolicy \

—policy-setting mode=Prevention

Attach it to the Application Gateway and associate with listeners or path-based rules.

DDoS Protection

Azure DDoS Protection is automatically included for platform services. For virtual networks, enable **DDoS Protection Standard** to protect against volumetric attacks.

Features:

- Always-on traffic monitoring
- Adaptive tuning
- Rapid attack mitigation
- Attack analytics and telemetry

```
az network ddos-protection create \
—resource-group MyRG \
—name DDoSProtectionPlan \
—location eastus
az network vnet update \
—name MyVNet \
—resource-group MyRG \
—ddos-protection-plan DDoSProtectionPlan \
—enable-ddos-protection true
```

Private Endpoints and Service Endpoints

Private Endpoints allow access to PaaS services over a private IP in your VNet, removing exposure to the public internet.

Example: Connect to Azure SQL via Private Endpoint

```
az network private-endpoint create \
—name SqlPrivateEndpoint \
—resource-group MyRG \
—vnet-name MyVNet \
—subnet MySubnet \
—private-connection-resource-id "/subscriptions/.../Microsoft.Sql/servers/myserver" \
—group-ids sqlServer \
—connection-name SqlPrivateConnection
```

Service Endpoints, in contrast, keep traffic within Azure's backbone network but are not fully private.

Use Private Endpoints when isolation is paramount (e.g., regulatory workloads).

Firewall Design Patterns

1. Hub-and-Spoke with Azure Firewall

- Centralized control of traffic

- Shared services live in hub (e.g., AD, DNS, Jumpbox)
- Application tiers live in spokes
- NSGs + Firewall rules + UDRs work in concert

2. Tiered Application with Segmented Subnets

- Web tier with WAF
- App tier behind NSGs
- DB tier accessible only from app subnet

3. VPN/ExpressRoute Termination with Perimeter Protection

- Terminate VPN in hub
- Filter inbound traffic via Azure Firewall before reaching workloads

---

Monitoring and Alerts

Use **Azure Monitor**, **Network Watcher**, and **Microsoft Defender for Cloud** to observe and protect network boundaries.

Sample NSG Flow Log KQL

```
AzureNetworkAnalytics_CL
| where FlowDirection_s == "Inbound"
| summarize count() by DestinationPort_d, RemoteIP_s
```

Set up alerts on suspicious ports (e.g., 3389, 22), unexpected traffic volume, or unauthorized source IPs.

Real-World Scenario: Financial Services Perimeter Design

A financial institution deploys sensitive workloads in Azure:

- **WAF-protected Application Gateway** for external APIs
- **Azure Firewall** enforces egress filtering and blocks known bad actors
- **Private Endpoints** for SQL, Blob, and Key Vault
- **NSGs** isolate dev/test/prod tiers
- **DDoS Protection** shields exposed IPs from volumetric attacks
- **VNet Peering** connects spokes to a central hub

This design achieves high security, compliance (e.g., PCI DSS), and fault isolation.

Summary

Perimeter security and network segmentation remain vital in securing modern cloud environments. Azure provides a comprehensive toolkit to design robust defenses against internal and external threats.

Key takeaways:

- Use **NSGs** for subnet- and NIC-level filtering
- Deploy **Azure Firewall** for centralized, stateful traffic control
- Protect web apps with **WAF on Application Gateway**
- Enable **DDoS Protection** for enhanced resilience
- Adopt **Private Endpoints** for secure PaaS access
- Monitor continuously with flow logs, alerts, and Defender for Cloud

These foundational elements enable secure-by-default Azure environments. The next section will focus on identity and access—implementing secure authentication and authorization practices across your cloud workloads.

Authentication and Authorization Best Practices

Authentication and authorization are foundational to securing applications and data in the cloud. While authentication answers the question "Who are you?", authorization determines "What can you do?". In Azure, these functions are centralized and managed through **Azure Active Directory (Azure AD)** and **Role-Based Access Control (RBAC)**, among other identity and access management tools. When implemented correctly, they form the front line of defense against data breaches, privilege escalation, and service misuse.

This section focuses on how to design robust, scalable, and maintainable authentication and authorization frameworks within

Azure. We'll examine identity models, access control mechanisms, zero trust principles, application integration, and monitoring strategies, all in the context of real-world architectures.

Identity Types in Azure

Understanding Azure identity types is the first step in applying proper access control:

Identity Type	Description
User	Human identity for employees or partners
Group	Collection of users, used for access assignment
Service Principal	Identity for applications or services (non-human)
Managed Identity	Azure-generated identity tied to a resource, used in automation and APIs
Guest User	External identity (e.g., B2B collaboration)

Each identity type plays a role in governing access to Azure resources and applications.

Authentication in Azure

Authentication verifies identity using credentials or tokens. Azure supports a wide range of authentication mechanisms:

- **Azure AD** for enterprise SSO and B2B access
- **OAuth 2.0 / OpenID Connect (OIDC)** for web and mobile apps
- **SAML 2.0** for legacy integrations

- **Certificate-based** or **federated** identity providers (IdPs)

- **Multi-Factor Authentication (MFA)** for elevated security

Enforcing MFA

MFA is essential for all privileged roles. Use Conditional Access to require MFA for:

- Admin roles

- High-risk users or sign-ins

- External IPs

```
az ad conditional-access policy create \
—name RequireMFAForAdmins \
—conditions "users=AdminGroup" \
—grant-controls "mfa"
```

Azure AD App Registration

Applications integrated with Azure AD require **app registration** for secure access:

- Register the app

- Define redirect URIs (e.g., https://myapp.com/auth/callback)

- Configure API permissions (e.g., Microsoft Graph, custom APIs)
- Use client secrets or certificates for confidential clients

Example: Registering an App via CLI

```
az ad app create \
—display-name "ContosoWebApp" \
—reply-urls "https://contoso.com/callback" \
—identifier-uris "https://contoso.com/webapp"
```

Tokens issued by Azure AD include claims about the user (e.g., roles, groups, tenant) and are used for authorization decisions in the app.

Authorization in Azure

Once identity is established, **authorization** controls access to resources. Azure primarily uses **Role-Based Access Control (RBAC)** to assign rights.

RBAC Components

- **Security Principal**: User, group, service principal, or managed identity
- **Role Definition**: Set of permissions (e.g., Reader, Contributor, Owner)
- **Scope**: Subscription, resource group, or resource

Assigning Roles

az role assignment create \

—assignee user@domain.com \

—role "Reader" \

—scope /subscriptions/{subId}/resourceGroups/{rgName}

Use **least privilege** principles—assign the minimum required role at the narrowest scope.

Built-In vs. Custom Roles

Azure provides built-in roles, but you can also define custom roles when fine-grained access control is needed.

Custom Role Example

{

"Name": "Blob Storage Reader",

"IsCustom": true,

"Description": "Read-only access to blob storage",

"Actions": [

"Microsoft.Storage/storageAccounts/blobServices/containers/read",

"Microsoft.Storage/storageAccounts/blobServices/containers/blobs/read"

],

```
"NotActions": [],
"AssignableScopes": ["/subscriptions/{subId}"]
}
```

Managed Identities for Services

Managed Identities allow Azure resources (e.g., VMs, Functions, Web Apps) to authenticate to Azure services without managing credentials.

Use Cases

- Accessing Azure Key Vault
- Writing to Azure Storage
- Querying Azure SQL or Cosmos DB

Enable System-Assigned Managed Identity

```
az webapp identity assign \
—name myWebApp \
—resource-group myRG
```

Grant access via RBAC:

```
az role assignment create \
—assignee <principalId> \
—role "Storage Blob Data Contributor" \
```

—scope /subscriptions/{subId}/resourceGroups/myRG/providers/Microsoft.Storage/storageAccounts/myStorage

---

Conditional Access

Conditional Access (CA) dynamically controls access based on user, location, device, and risk.

Examples

- Block sign-ins from outside approved countries
- Require MFA for external identities
- Restrict access to compliant devices (via Intune)

Policy Example: Block Legacy Authentication

az ad conditional-access policy create \

—name BlockLegacyAuth \

—conditions "client-app-types=Other" \

—grant-controls "block"

Just-in-Time Access and PIM

Use **Azure AD Privileged Identity Management (PIM)** to reduce standing privileges:

- Time-bound access to critical roles
- Approval workflows

- MFA enforcement
- Notifications and audit logs

PIM Benefits

- Reduces insider threat risks
- Minimizes attack surface
- Provides visibility into privileged activity

Application-Level Authorization

Applications should enforce their own access rules, using:

- **Claims-based Authorization**: Extract roles or group memberships from JWT
- **Policy-Based Access Control (PBAC)**: Evaluate dynamic conditions
- **Attribute-Based Access Control (ABAC)**: Evaluate context, location, device, time

Claims Extraction Example

```
if (user.claims.roles.includes("Admin")) {
allowAccess();
} else {
denyAccess();
```

}

Monitoring and Auditing Identity Activity

Azure logs all authentication and access events. Use:

- **Sign-in logs**: Track login attempts and failures
- **Audit logs**: Track role assignments and app usage
- **Azure Monitor & Log Analytics**: Build alerts and dashboards
- **Defender for Identity**: Detect suspicious behavior and insider threats

KQL: Failed Sign-Ins

```
SigninLogs
| where ResultType != 0
| summarize count() by UserPrincipalName, ResultDescription
```

Set alerts for high-failure accounts or sign-ins from unexpected countries.

Real-World Scenario: Securing a Healthcare App

A healthcare SaaS platform uses Azure AD and RBAC to enforce strict data access controls:

- **Azure AD B2C** for patient authentication
- **RBAC** and **Custom Roles** for doctor vs. admin privileges

- **Managed Identity** for accessing protected health info in Azure Storage
- **Conditional Access** to require MFA for out-of-network access
- **Privileged Identity Management** for support engineers
- **Sign-in logs** integrated into **SIEM** for compliance reporting (e.g., HIPAA)

This ensures secure, compliant identity and access handling across a multi-tenant, regulated environment.

Summary

Authentication and authorization form the backbone of cloud security. Azure offers enterprise-grade tools to verify identity, manage access, and enforce policy across applications and services.

Key takeaways:

- Use **Azure AD** for centralized identity and access control
- Apply **RBAC** using least privilege principles
- Integrate **Managed Identities** to eliminate secrets
- Leverage **Conditional Access** for adaptive, real-time policies
- Use **PIM** to control privileged role assignment

- Monitor identity usage and automate threat response

The next section will cover **Data Protection and Key Management**, focusing on how to encrypt, store, and manage sensitive data securely across the Azure ecosystem.

Data Protection and Key Management

Data protection is a critical pillar of cloud security, encompassing encryption, key management, access control, and secure storage practices. In Azure, organizations are responsible for protecting data at rest, in transit, and in use. With the rise of privacy regulations such as GDPR, HIPAA, and CCPA, the need to manage encryption keys, prevent data leakage, and control access has become more important than ever.

Azure offers a wide array of services and features for protecting data, including **Azure Key Vault**, **Azure Storage encryption**, **SQL Transparent Data Encryption (TDE)**, **Customer-Managed Keys (CMK)**, **Managed HSM**, and **Azure Confidential Computing**. In this section, we will explore these services and present a comprehensive strategy for safeguarding sensitive data in the cloud.

Core Principles of Data Protection

1. **Data Classification**: Identify and tag sensitive data based on its importance and regulatory requirements.
2. **Encryption**: Always encrypt sensitive data at rest, in transit, and optionally in use.
3. **Key Management**: Centralize key storage and enforce strict access policies.
4. **Separation of Duties**: Ensure that those who manage infrastructure cannot access encrypted data.

5. **Audit and Monitor**: Track access to sensitive data and key usage through detailed logs and alerts.

Encryption at Rest in Azure

Azure encrypts data at rest by default using **Storage Service Encryption (SSE)** and **Azure Disk Encryption (ADE)**. For most services, Azure manages the keys automatically (**Microsoft-managed keys**, MMK), but you can opt for **Customer-managed keys** (CMK) for greater control.

Services with Built-in Encryption at Rest

- **Azure Blob Storage**
- **Azure File Storage**
- **Azure Disks**
- **Azure SQL Database**
- **Cosmos DB**
- **Azure Synapse Analytics**

```
az storage account update \
—name mystorageaccount \
—resource-group myRG \
—encryption-key-source Microsoft.Keyvault \
—key-name mykey \
```

—key-vault-uri https://myvault.vault.azure.net/

This command enables CMK for a storage account using a key in Azure Key Vault.

Encryption in Transit

All Azure services support **TLS 1.2** encryption for data in transit. For internal traffic within VNets or hybrid networks, encryption can be enforced using **VPNs**, **ExpressRoute encryption**, or **Private Link**.

Best practices:

- Disable older protocols (SSL 3.0, TLS 1.0/1.1)
- Enforce HTTPS-only access for web services
- Use Azure Front Door or Application Gateway for SSL termination

---

Azure Key Vault

Azure Key Vault is the foundation of key and secret management in Azure. It supports:

- **Key storage** (RSA, EC, symmetric keys)
- **Secrets** (passwords, connection strings, tokens)
- **Certificates** (imported or generated)
- **Managed HSM** (FIPS 140-2 Level 3 compliance)

Key Vault Access Control

Key Vault supports two models:

- **Vault Access Policy**: Legacy, static role assignments
- **Azure RBAC**: Recommended model for fine-grained and auditable access

```
az keyvault create \
—name myVault \
—resource-group myRG \
—enable-rbac-authorization true
```

Assign access using standard roles:

- Key Vault Reader
- Key Vault Secrets User
- Key Vault Crypto Service Encryption User

Using Keys in Applications

Applications can use **Managed Identities** to authenticate to Key Vault without secrets.

```
const { DefaultAzureCredential } = require("@azure/identity");
const { SecretClient } = require("@azure/keyvault-secrets");
const credential = new DefaultAzureCredential();
```

const client = new SecretClient("https://myvault.vault.azure.net", credential);

const secret = await client.getSecret("DbConnectionString");

This method avoids embedding secrets in code or config files.

Customer-Managed Keys (CMK)

CMKs offer greater control over encryption keys and their lifecycle. They are stored in Key Vault and linked to Azure resources such as:

- **Storage Accounts**
- **SQL Databases**
- **Azure Kubernetes Service (AKS) Secrets**
- **Azure Cognitive Services**

Use CMK when:

- Required by compliance (HIPAA, FedRAMP)
- You want to rotate, disable, or revoke keys
- Separation of responsibilities is needed between data owners and operators

az sql server key create \

—resource-group myRG \

—server myserver \

—kid https://myvault.vault.azure.net/keys/mykey/1234567890abcdef

Key Rotation and Expiry

To ensure long-term security, rotate keys regularly:

- **Set key expiration** in Key Vault
- Use **soft delete** and **purge protection** to prevent accidental loss
- Automate rotation using Azure Functions or Logic Apps

Key Expiry Alert (KQL)

```
AzureDiagnostics
| where ResourceType == "VAULTS" and OperationName == "SecretGet"
| where ResultType == "Success"
| summarize count() by Resource, bin(TimeGenerated, 1d)
```

Hardware Security Modules (HSM)

For ultra-sensitive data, use **Azure Key Vault Managed HSM**:

- Fully isolated HSM-backed key storage
- FIPS 140-2 Level 3 certified
- Bring your own HSM keys (BYOK)
- Managed via RBAC

```
az keyvault create \
```

—name myManagedHSM \

—resource-group myRG \

—location eastus \

—hsm-name myhsm \

—enable-rbac-authorization true

Managed HSM is ideal for finance, healthcare, and government applications requiring strict cryptographic boundary assurance.

Confidential Computing

Azure Confidential Computing allows data to be processed in encrypted memory, using **Trusted Execution Environments (TEEs)**:

- Leverages Intel SGX hardware
- Protects data while in use
- Available on specific VM SKUs (e.g., DC-series)

Use cases include:

- Encrypted data analytics
- Blockchain processing
- Secure ML inference

Auditing and Monitoring

Track key and secret access using:

- **Key Vault diagnostic logs**
- **Azure Monitor**
- **Microsoft Defender for Cloud**
- **Log Analytics and KQL**

Track Key Usage

```
AzureDiagnostics
| where ResourceType == "VAULTS"
| where OperationName contains "KeyOperation"
| summarize count() by Identity, OperationName, bin(TimeGenerated, 1h)
```

Set alerts on unexpected access patterns or privilege escalations.

Real-World Scenario: FinTech Key Management Strategy

A FinTech platform handles sensitive financial data and requires strict key control:

- **Customer-managed keys** protect blob storage and databases
- **Azure Key Vault** stores API secrets and database credentials
- **Managed identities** grant secure access to apps and pipelines

- **Key rotation** scheduled every 90 days
- **Managed HSM** protects root signing keys for payment authorizations
- All access logs streamed to **SIEM** for compliance (PCI DSS, SOC 2)

This layered strategy enables compliance, mitigates risk, and supports scalability across the organization.

Summary

Data protection and key management are non-negotiable in a secure Azure architecture. By encrypting data, centralizing key control, and enforcing strong access policies, organizations can safeguard their most critical assets.

Key takeaways:

- Encrypt data at rest and in transit using default or customer-managed keys
- Use **Azure Key Vault** and **Managed HSM** to manage keys, secrets, and certs
- Enforce **Azure RBAC** for secure access control
- Integrate **Managed Identities** to eliminate plaintext credentials
- Monitor and rotate keys regularly to prevent compromise

- Leverage **Confidential Computing** to protect data during processing

The next section will explore **Secure DevOps with Azure DevSecOps**, ensuring that security is integrated across the software development lifecycle.

Secure DevOps with Azure DevSecOps

The integration of security practices into every phase of the software development lifecycle is no longer optional—it is a necessity. As organizations increasingly embrace DevOps for faster release cycles, they must also adopt **DevSecOps** to ensure that security is not an afterthought but a fundamental component of the development pipeline. In Azure, Secure DevOps—or **DevSecOps**—is implemented through a blend of automation, policy enforcement, compliance validation, and security tooling built directly into the cloud ecosystem.

Azure provides a rich suite of services and tools to embed security into your CI/CD pipelines, infrastructure provisioning, code management, container workflows, and runtime environments. These include **Azure DevOps**, **GitHub Actions**, **Microsoft Defender for Cloud**, **Azure Policy**, **Azure Blueprints**, and **Security Center integrations**.

This section explores how to build a secure development workflow in Azure—from planning and development to release and operations—ensuring that vulnerabilities are caught early, infrastructure is compliant, and applications are resilient against threats.

DevSecOps Principles

1. **Shift Left**: Integrate security early in the development cycle, not just during deployment.
2. **Security as Code**: Treat security policies, configurations, and validations as version-controlled code.
3. **Automation First**: Automate security scanning, compliance enforcement, and policy validation.
4. **Continuous Monitoring**: Apply ongoing visibility into code, infrastructure, and workloads.
5. **Least Privilege**: Ensure users and services only have the permissions they absolutely need.
6. **Security Ownership**: Empower development teams to own and fix security issues autonomously.

Secure CI/CD Pipelines with Azure DevOps

Azure DevOps allows you to build secure pipelines that automatically scan code, validate infrastructure, and enforce security gates.

Key Integration Points

- **Static Application Security Testing (SAST)** for code quality and vulnerabilities
- **Secrets detection** for hardcoded credentials
- **Container vulnerability scanning**
- **Infrastructure as Code (IaC) validation** with tools like Terraform, Bicep, or ARM

- **Approval gates** for critical changes
- **Azure Policy and Security Center integration**

Sample YAML Pipeline with Security Tasks

```
trigger:
- main
jobs:
- job: Build
steps:
- task: UseDotNet@2
inputs:
packageType: 'sdk'
version: '6.x'
- task: DotNetCoreCLI@2
inputs:
command: 'build'
projects: '**/*.csproj'
- task: SonarQubePrepare@4
inputs:
SonarQube: 'SonarCloud'
projectKey: 'my-app'
```

projectName: 'My App'

- task: SonarQubeAnalyze@4

- task: SonarQubePublish@4

inputs:

pollingTimeoutSec: '300'

Use SonarCloud, Snyk, Whitesource, or similar tools to integrate security checks.

GitHub Actions and Security Automation

If you're using GitHub, security automation is also deeply integrated through **GitHub Advanced Security**, **Dependabot**, **CodeQL**, and third-party marketplace actions.

Example: Security Workflow for a Node.js App

name: Security Scan

on: [push]

jobs:

scan:

runs-on: ubuntu-latest

steps:

- uses: actions/checkout@v2

- uses: github/codeql-action/init@v2

with:

languages: javascript

- uses: github/codeql-action/analyze@v2

This setup checks code for vulnerabilities automatically on each push.

Secrets Management in DevSecOps

Hardcoding credentials in code or pipelines is one of the most common and dangerous mistakes. Azure DevSecOps workflows should rely on **Azure Key Vault** to store secrets securely.

Secure Access in Pipelines

- task: AzureKeyVault@2

inputs:

connectedServiceName: 'AzureSPN'

keyVaultName: 'myKeyVault'

secretsFilter: 'DbPassword,ApiKey'

Applications and pipelines should use **Managed Identities** to retrieve secrets dynamically, avoiding manual secret injection or exposure.

Infrastructure as Code Security

Infrastructure code (ARM, Bicep, Terraform) must be validated for security best practices.

Tools and Techniques

- **TFSec**: Static analysis for Terraform
- **Checkov**: Scans Terraform, CloudFormation, Kubernetes, etc.
- **Bicep linter**: Flags misconfigurations in Bicep templates
- **Azure Policy**: Enforce configuration standards in deployment

Example: TFSec Scan in Pipeline

```
- script: |
tfsec ./infrastructure
displayName: 'Run tfsec'
```

Combine IaC scans with Azure Policy assignments to block non-compliant deployments automatically.

Container Security in Azure DevSecOps

For teams using Kubernetes or containerized deployments, it's critical to:

- **Scan container images** for vulnerabilities
- Use **base images from trusted registries**
- Enable **runtime protections** in AKS

Azure Container Registry (ACR) Integration

- Enable **Microsoft Defender for Containers** to scan images on push
- Reject images that fail security checks
- Integrate with CI/CD to fail builds on CVEs

az acr update—name myacr—resource-group myRG—anonymous-pull-enabled false

Use tools like **Trivy**, **Clair**, or **Anchore** for custom image scans in CI pipelines.

Azure Policy and Blueprints

Azure Policy is essential for enforcing security standards across resources. Apply policies that:

- Require encryption at rest
- Block public IPs on sensitive resources
- Enforce tagging for cost and ownership
- Require diagnostic logs

Sample Policy: Deny Public IPs

{

"if": {

"field": "Microsoft.Network/publicIPAddresses/ipAddress",

```
"exists": "true"
},
"then": {
"effect": "deny"
}
}
```

Deploy via **Azure Blueprints** to combine policy assignments, RBAC roles, and ARM templates.

Microsoft Defender for Cloud

Microsoft Defender for Cloud continuously monitors your environment and provides:

- Secure score recommendations
- Regulatory compliance mappings (ISO, PCI, NIST, etc.)
- Threat detection for VMs, containers, and databases
- Integration with Sentinel for SIEM functionality

Use Defender as a feedback loop for your DevSecOps practices—each finding is an opportunity to automate remediations.

Monitoring and Alerting in DevSecOps

Security issues need to trigger alerts and dashboards:

- **Azure Monitor**: Central platform for metrics and logs

- **Log Analytics**: Write KQL queries for real-time insights
- **Alerts**: Notify engineers on high-severity issues
- **Azure Sentinel**: Correlate logs and run playbooks for automated response

Example: Alert for Secret Access

```
AzureDiagnostics
| where OperationName == "SecretGet" and ResultType != "Success"
| summarize count() by Identity, Resource, bin(TimeGenerated, 1h)
```

Real-World Scenario: Secure DevOps for Healthcare SaaS

A healthcare SaaS provider builds DevSecOps pipelines in Azure to meet HIPAA requirements:

- **Azure DevOps** with integrated SAST, IaC linting, and container scans
- **Key Vault** for secret storage, used by pipelines and apps
- **Azure Policy** enforces encryption and disallows public resources
- **PIM and RBAC** ensure least privilege access to repos and environments

- **Defender for Cloud** and **Sentinel** alert on anomalies and compliance drift

This approach enables fast iteration while maintaining a hardened security posture.

Summary

Secure DevOps in Azure requires the seamless integration of security into every development stage. By automating checks, enforcing policies, and equipping developers with security tools, organizations can reduce risk without compromising speed.

Key takeaways:

- Integrate **security scanning** in CI/CD using Azure DevOps or GitHub Actions

- Manage **secrets securely** with Azure Key Vault and Managed Identities

- Apply **IaC validation** and enforce standards with **Azure Policy**

- Scan **container images** and implement runtime protection in AKS

- Use **Defender for Cloud** for continuous visibility and risk mitigation

- Monitor security posture with **KQL, Azure Monitor, and Sentinel**

Security is not a phase—it's a practice. With Azure DevSecOps, you can build resilient, compliant, and fast-moving development pipelines that scale confidently in the cloud.

Chapter 7: Resiliency and Monitoring Patterns

Retry and Circuit Breaker Patterns

Modern cloud applications are distributed by nature, involving numerous microservices, APIs, databases, third-party integrations, and messaging systems. While this modular approach provides scalability and agility, it also introduces failure points. Services may become temporarily unavailable due to transient errors, network issues, throttling, or maintenance. To build robust systems that can recover gracefully from such failures, developers rely on **resiliency patterns**, especially **retry** and **circuit breaker**.

This section delves deep into the principles, design, and implementation of the Retry and Circuit Breaker patterns in Azure-based applications. We'll also look at when and how to use them, recommended libraries, configuration guidelines, and integrations with Azure services.

The Need for Resiliency

Even the most reliable cloud services can occasionally fail. These failures are often transient and recoverable if retried after a short delay. However, aggressive retrying or ignoring failures altogether can cause:

- Exacerbation of the failure (e.g., retry storms)
- Resource exhaustion
- User frustration

- Data inconsistency

Resiliency patterns help prevent these outcomes by enabling **graceful degradation**, **self-healing**, and **fault isolation**.

Retry Pattern

The Retry pattern enables an application to handle transient failures by retrying an operation after a delay. The retries can be immediate or delayed using a **backoff strategy**.

Common Scenarios for Retry

- Network timeouts
- Rate-limiting (HTTP 429 Too Many Requests)
- Temporary unavailability of a downstream service (HTTP 503)
- Database transient faults

Backoff Strategies

- **Fixed Interval**: Retry after a constant delay (e.g., 5 seconds)
- **Exponential Backoff**: Wait time doubles after each attempt (e.g., 1s, 2s, 4s, 8s...)
- **Jitter**: Adds randomness to delay to avoid thundering herd problem

Implementing Retry in Azure Applications

.NET with Polly

Polly[1] is a powerful .NET resilience and transient-fault-handling library.

```
var retryPolicy = Policy

.Handle<HttpRequestException>()

.OrResult<HttpResponseMessage>(r => !r.IsSuccessStatusCode)

.WaitAndRetryAsync(3, retryAttempt =>

TimeSpan.FromSeconds(Math.Pow(2, retryAttempt))

);

await retryPolicy.ExecuteAsync(() => httpClient.GetAsync("https://api.example.com"));
```

Azure SDK Retry Configuration

Most Azure SDKs have built-in retry policies.

```
var options = new BlobClientOptions

{

Retry =

{

Mode = RetryMode.Exponential,
```

1. https://github.com/App-vNext/Polly

```
MaxRetries = 5,
Delay = TimeSpan.FromSeconds(2),
MaxDelay = TimeSpan.FromSeconds(30)
}
};
```

Enable retries in:

- Cosmos DB SDK
- Azure Storage SDK
- Azure Service Bus SDK

Logic Apps and Durable Functions

Azure Logic Apps have built-in retry policies:

```
{
"retryPolicy": {
"type": "exponential",
"interval": "PT5S",
"count": 3
}
}
```

Durable Functions automatically retry failed activities unless overridden.

Circuit Breaker Pattern

The Circuit Breaker pattern prevents an application from performing operations likely to fail. When a threshold of failures is reached, the circuit is "tripped" into an **open state**, short-circuiting further attempts for a defined duration.

Circuit States

- **Closed**: Normal operation. All requests are attempted.
- **Open**: Requests are immediately failed without executing.
- **Half-Open**: A limited number of test requests are allowed to probe system health.

Benefits

- Prevents system overload
- Gives failing services time to recover
- Avoids cascading failures
- Improves user experience with fast failure

Implementing Circuit Breaker

Polly Circuit Breaker

var breaker = Policy

```
.Handle<HttpRequestException>()
.CircuitBreakerAsync(
exceptionsAllowedBeforeBreaking: 3,
durationOfBreak: TimeSpan.FromSeconds(30)
);
try
{
await breaker.ExecuteAsync(() => httpClient.GetAsync("https://api.example.com"));
}
catch (BrokenCircuitException)
{
Console.WriteLine("Circuit is open - skipping call.");
}
```

Azure API Management Integration

Use **APIM policies** to implement retry and circuit breaker logic at the gateway level.

```
<retry condition="@(context.Response.StatusCode == 500)" count="3" interval="2" />
```

For circuit breaking, combine API Management with Azure Functions or custom code that maintains state in Redis or Cosmos DB.

Real-World Patterns with Azure Services

Cosmos DB Retry

Cosmos DB supports automatic retries for **429 (Rate Limited)** responses with exponential backoff.

Azure Service Bus

The SDK retries transient failures, and **dead-lettering** handles persistent ones. You can also add custom retry policies in message handlers.

Azure Functions

Use Durable Functions with **RetryOptions** to retry activities.

RetryOptions retryOptions = new RetryOptions(TimeSpan.FromSeconds(5), 3);

await context.CallActivityWithRetryAsync("ProcessOrder", retryOptions, order);

Monitoring and Alerting

Use **Azure Monitor** and **Application Insights** to track resiliency patterns in real-time.

Key Metrics

- Retry counts and success/failure rates

- Circuit breaker status
- Latency patterns
- Dependency health

Sample KQL to Monitor Retries

```
traces

| where message contains "Retrying"

| summarize count() by operation_Name, bin(timestamp, 5m)
```

Set alerts when retries spike abnormally—this may indicate a systemic issue.

Design Considerations

- **Don't retry non-transient errors**: e.g., 400 Bad Request
- **Limit max retry count**: to avoid infinite loops
- **Use idempotent operations**: so retries don't cause data corruption
- **Log retry attempts**: for diagnostics and performance tuning
- **Consider fallback policies**: to gracefully degrade functionality

---

Real-World Scenario: E-Commerce API Resilience

An e-commerce platform uses Azure to host its microservices. The order processing service calls a payment API that occasionally throttles requests.

- **Retry Pattern**: Polly handles transient HTTP 429s with jittered exponential backoff.
- **Circuit Breaker**: Trips after 5 consecutive failures; opens circuit for 1 minute.
- **Fallback**: Caches response from a mock service when the circuit is open.
- **Application Insights** tracks retry metrics and circuit breaker transitions.
- **APIM** has retry logic for public endpoints, protecting backend APIs.

This ensures the system stays responsive even during third-party outages.

Summary

The Retry and Circuit Breaker patterns are essential to building resilient cloud-native applications. By anticipating failure and designing for graceful recovery, you can maintain service availability and ensure a better user experience.

Key takeaways:

- Use the **Retry Pattern** for transient fault handling with backoff strategies.

- Apply the **Circuit Breaker Pattern** to isolate and prevent cascading failures.
- Implement these patterns in **code**, **APIM**, or **Durable Functions**.
- Monitor retry and circuit states using **Azure Monitor** and **Application Insights**.
- Always design retries with **idempotency**, **timeouts**, and **fallbacks** in mind.

The next section will cover monitoring patterns using Azure Monitor and Application Insights to detect, diagnose, and respond to operational issues effectively.

Monitoring with Azure Monitor and Application Insights

Observability is fundamental to operating and maintaining reliable cloud-native applications. In a distributed Azure environment, where microservices, databases, APIs, queues, and serverless functions interact across dynamic infrastructure, having real-time insight into system health, performance, and user behavior is essential.

Azure provides powerful observability services through **Azure Monitor** and **Application Insights**, which together offer deep visibility across applications and infrastructure. Whether you need to track errors, analyze usage, detect anomalies, or trace complex operations across services, these tools deliver comprehensive insights to support DevOps, SRE, and security teams.

This section explores how to implement a robust monitoring strategy using Azure-native tools, ensuring your applications remain performant, resilient, and user-centric.

Observability Pillars

Modern monitoring in Azure revolves around the three core pillars of observability:

1. **Logs** – Detailed records of events (e.g., application logs, audit logs, diagnostic logs)
2. **Metrics** – Quantitative data (e.g., CPU usage, request rate, error count)
3. **Traces** – End-to-end request flows across distributed components

Azure Monitor and Application Insights integrate these pillars into a unified platform.

Azure Monitor Overview

Azure Monitor is the platform-wide monitoring service that collects and analyzes telemetry from Azure resources, custom applications, and on-premises systems.

Key Capabilities

- Collection of **metrics** and **logs**
- **Alerts** and automated actions
- **Dashboards** and visualizations
- **Workbooks** for custom reports

- **Log Analytics** with KQL
- Integration with **Azure Defender**, **Sentinel**, and **Logic Apps**

Use Azure Monitor for infrastructure observability, platform metrics, and operational intelligence.

Application Insights Overview

Application Insights is an application performance management (APM) service that collects detailed telemetry from running applications.

Supported Platforms

- ASP.NET Core, Java, Node.js, Python, and more
- Azure Functions, App Services, AKS
- Front-end frameworks via JavaScript SDK

Key Features

- Automatic request logging and performance tracking
- Exception and dependency monitoring
- Live metrics stream
- Distributed tracing
- Usage analytics and funnel conversion tracking

Configuring Monitoring for Azure Resources

Enable Diagnostics for Azure Services

Example: Enable logging for an Azure App Service

az monitor diagnostic-settings create \

—resource /subscriptions/{id}/resourceGroups/myRG/providers/Microsoft.Web/sites/myApp \

—name "AppDiagnostics" \

—workspace "/subscriptions/{id}/resourceGroups/myRG/providers/Microsoft.OperationalInsights/workspaces/myLogAnalytics" \

—logs '[{"category": "AppServiceHTTPLogs", "enabled": true}]' \

—metrics '[{"category": "AllMetrics", "enabled": true}]'

Send logs to Log Analytics, Event Hub, or Storage for persistence and analysis.

Application Insights in Action

Auto-Instrumentation

For Azure App Services, simply enable Application Insights from the portal—no code changes required.

SDK-Based Instrumentation

.NET Example:

```
services.AddApplicationInsightsTelemetry(Configuration["ApplicationIns
```

JavaScript Example (client-side):

```
<script type="text/javascript">

var appInsights = window.appInsights || function (config) {

function r(config) { t[config] = function () { var i = arguments; t.queue.push(function () { t[config].apply(t, i) }) } }

var t = { config: config }, u = document, e = window, o = "script", s = u.createElement(o), i, f;

for (s.src = config.url || "https://az416426.vo.msecnd.net/scripts/b/ai.2.min.js", u.getElementsByTagName(o)[0].parentNode.appendChild(s), t.cookie = u.cookie, t.queue = [], i = ["trackEvent", "trackPageView", "trackException", "trackTrace", "trackMetric", "trackDependency", "setAuthenticatedUserContext", "clearAuthenticatedUserContext", "flush"], f = 0; f < i.length; f++) r(i[f]);

return t;

}({

instrumentationKey: "YOUR_INSTRUMENTATION_KEY"

});

window.appInsights = appInsights;

appInsights.trackPageView();

</script>
```

Distributed Tracing

Distributed tracing allows you to follow a request across microservices and visualize its entire journey.

- Automatically enabled in Azure Functions, App Service, AKS
- Correlates telemetry between services (dependencies, requests, and exceptions)
- Uses **operation_Id** to stitch trace spans

Example Trace in KQL

```
traces

| where operation_Id == "d1a9c31df7b3452aa2f90e4b1f8fa9c4"

| order by timestamp asc
```

Visualize traces in the **Application Map** for root cause analysis.

Custom Events and Metrics

Use custom telemetry to track business KPIs or custom app behavior.

```
var telemetry = new TelemetryClient();

telemetry.TrackEvent("UserSignedUp", new Dictionary<string, string>

{

{ "plan", "premium" },
```

{ "region", "UK" }

});

Define custom **metrics** (e.g., "OrdersPlaced", "CheckoutFailures") and **dimensions** (e.g., region, customer type).

Alerts and Automation

Azure Monitor supports **metric alerts**, **log-based alerts**, and **smart detection** (anomaly-based alerts in App Insights).

Example: Alert on CPU Usage > 80%

az monitor metrics alert create \

—name "HighCPUAlert" \

—resource-group myRG \

—scopes "/subscriptions/{id}/resourceGroups/myRG/providers/Microsoft.Compute/virtualMachines/myVM" \

—condition "avg Percentage CPU > 80" \

—window-size 5m \

—evaluation-frequency 1m \

—action "/subscriptions/{id}/resourceGroups/myRG/providers/microsoft.insights/actionGroups/myActionGroup"

Alerts can trigger emails, SMS, Logic Apps, Azure Functions, or ITSM systems.

Workbooks and Dashboards

Use **Azure Workbooks** to build interactive visual reports using KQL queries, metrics, and visualizations.

Example: App Performance Overview

- Requests by region
- Average response time per endpoint
- Error rate over time
- Funnel analysis: Signup → Profile Complete → Purchase

Dashboards can combine metrics across services for NOC-style visibility.

Real-World Scenario: SaaS Observability Stack

A global SaaS provider runs multiple microservices in Azure Kubernetes Service (AKS) with APIs, databases, and queues.

- **Application Insights** tracks request latency and availability per service
- **Azure Monitor** tracks pod CPU/memory, disk usage, and scaling metrics
- **Distributed tracing** maps all request flows through APIs and background workers
- **Custom metrics** capture business KPIs (logins, conversions, failed payments)

- **Log Analytics** alerts on exception spikes and query response degradation

- Workbooks visualize system health by tenant, environment, and SLA tier

This full-stack observability enables proactive issue detection, reduced MTTR, and data-driven service improvement.

Summary

Monitoring and observability are critical to operating resilient and performant applications in Azure. With Azure Monitor and Application Insights, you gain powerful capabilities to detect issues, analyze trends, and maintain system integrity.

Key takeaways:

- **Azure Monitor** collects and analyzes platform and resource telemetry.

- **Application Insights** provides deep APM and usage analytics.

- Use **distributed tracing** to debug across microservices.

- Create **alerts**, **dashboards**, and **workbooks** for actionable insights.

- Automate responses with **Logic Apps** and **Azure Functions**.

- Track both **technical** and **business** metrics to optimize operations.

The next section will explore auto-scaling and failover patterns, ensuring systems can adapt to load and recover gracefully from disruptions.

Auto-Scaling and Failover Designs

In cloud-native architecture, scalability and high availability are not luxuries—they are baseline requirements. Systems must handle varying loads gracefully while maintaining uptime even in the face of failures. Auto-scaling and failover mechanisms ensure that applications remain performant under pressure and resilient to infrastructure outages.

Azure offers a rich set of features to automatically scale resources and failover to alternate regions or systems. These include **Azure Virtual Machine Scale Sets**, **App Service Autoscale**, **AKS horizontal pod autoscaling**, **Traffic Manager**, **Availability Zones**, **Geo-redundant Storage**, and **Azure Front Door**.

This section explores how to design robust auto-scaling and failover strategies in Azure. We will review patterns, services, configurations, and operational considerations to help you build responsive and highly available systems.

Auto-Scaling: Core Concepts

Auto-scaling is the dynamic adjustment of compute resources to meet changing demand. It ensures optimal performance during traffic spikes and cost-efficiency during low usage.

Types of Scaling

- **Vertical Scaling**: Increasing the size (CPU/RAM) of a single instance (e.g., upgrading a VM SKU)

- **Horizontal Scaling**: Adding/removing instances (e.g., more VMs or containers)

Azure favors **horizontal scaling** due to its support for distributed, stateless workloads.

Scaling Metrics

Auto-scaling decisions are based on:

- CPU or memory usage
- Request count or throughput
- Queue length
- Custom metrics (e.g., concurrent users)

Autoscale with Azure App Services

Azure App Service provides built-in autoscale for web apps.

Steps to Configure Autoscale

1. Enable scaling in the App Service Plan (must be Standard tier or above).
2. Set rules for scaling out/in based on metrics.

az monitor autoscale create \

—resource-group myRG \

—resource /subscriptions/{id}/resourceGroups/myRG/providers/Microsoft.Web/serverfarms/myAppPlan \

—name "AutoScaleAppService"

az monitor autoscale rule create \

—autoscale-name "AutoScaleAppService" \

—resource-group myRG \

—metric-name "CpuPercentage" \

—condition "GreaterThan 70 avg 5m" \

—scale out 1

This rule scales out when CPU usage exceeds 70% for 5 minutes.

Azure Virtual Machine Scale Sets (VMSS)

VMSS allow you to deploy and manage a set of identical VMs that automatically scale based on load.

VMSS Features

- Auto-balancing across Availability Zones
- Custom image support
- Integration with Azure Load Balancer
- Supports Spot VMs and mixed-priority configurations

az vmss create \

—resource-group myRG \

—name myScaleSet \

—image UbuntuLTS \

—upgrade-policy-mode automatic \

—admin-username azureuser \

—generate-ssh-keys

Configure autoscale with rules for metrics like CPU or queue depth from Azure Service Bus.

Kubernetes (AKS) Horizontal Pod Autoscaler (HPA)

In AKS, the Horizontal Pod Autoscaler adjusts the number of pod replicas based on resource consumption.

apiVersion: autoscaling/v2

kind: HorizontalPodAutoscaler

metadata:

name: my-hpa

spec:

scaleTargetRef:

apiVersion: apps/v1

kind: Deployment

name: my-deployment

minReplicas: 2

maxReplicas: 10

metrics:

- type: Resource

resource:

name: cpu

target:

type: Utilization

averageUtilization: 70

You can also autoscale based on custom metrics using the Kubernetes Metrics Server or Prometheus Adapter.

Azure Functions Auto-Scaling

Azure Functions in the **consumption plan** scale automatically based on trigger events. For example, an HTTP-triggered function may scale out to handle thousands of concurrent requests.

For **premium plans**, you can configure minimum and maximum instance counts for better control.

Scale Triggers

- HTTP requests
- Queue length (Azure Storage Queues, Service Bus)
- Timer-based triggers

Azure handles the scaling infrastructure; developers only need to ensure stateless function design.

Failover Design Patterns

While auto-scaling improves performance, **failover** ensures availability when components fail.

Azure Failover Building Blocks

Component	Feature
Azure Front Door	Global load balancing with health probes
Traffic Manager	DNS-based regional failover
Availability Zones	Fault domain isolation within a region
Availability Sets	VM-level fault domain separation
GEO Redundancy	Backup and replication to secondary regions

Azure Front Door for Active-Active Failover

Azure Front Door distributes global traffic across multiple backend regions.

- Uses health probes to detect outages
- Routes traffic to the closest healthy endpoint
- Supports custom routing rules and WAF integration

Sample Routing Setup

```
{
"backends": [
{ "address": "app-eastus.azurewebsites.net", "priority": 1 },
{ "address": "app-westeurope.azurewebsites.net", "priority": 2 }
```

```
]
}
```

Traffic Manager for Passive Failover

Traffic Manager is DNS-based and checks health before routing traffic.

Routing Methods

- Priority: Primary + backup
- Weighted: Load balancing
- Geographic: Route by location
- Performance: Route by lowest latency

```
az network traffic-manager profile create \
—name myProfile \
—resource-group myRG \
—routing-method Priority \
—unique-dns-name myapp \
—ttl 30 \
—monitor-path "/" \
—monitor-port 80 \
—monitor-protocol HTTP
```

Storage and Database Failover

Azure offers **geo-redundant storage** (**GRS**) and **read-access GRS** (**RA-GRS**) for automatic replication to a secondary region.

- **Cosmos DB**: Multi-region writes and auto-failover
- **Azure SQL Database**: Active geo-replication with auto-failover groups
- **Blob Storage**: Geo-zone redundant storage (GZRS) for regional disaster protection

Cosmos DB Example

```
az cosmosdb create \
—name myCosmosDb \
—resource-group myRG \
—locations regionName=eastus failoverPriority=0 \
—locations regionName=westeurope failoverPriority=1 \
—enable-automatic-failover true
```

Monitoring Auto-Scaling and Failover Events

Use Azure Monitor to track scaling activity and detect failovers.

KQL to Track Scale Events

```
AzureDiagnostics
| where ResourceType == "AUTOSCALESETTINGS"
```

| where OperationName contains "Scale"

| project TimeGenerated, OperationName, ResultType

Alerts

- Alert when max instance count is hit (may indicate under-provisioning)
- Alert on region outage detected by Front Door or Traffic Manager
- Track SLA compliance per region

Real-World Scenario: Global E-Commerce Platform

A large e-commerce site operates in North America and Europe:

- **AKS clusters** in East US and West Europe
- **Azure Front Door** routes traffic based on latency and availability
- **Auto-scaling** ensures backend services can handle Black Friday traffic spikes
- **Azure Cosmos DB** with multi-region writes for global inventory data
- **Geo-redundant storage** protects order receipts
- Failures automatically shift traffic and workloads with near-zero downtime

This architecture supports tens of thousands of concurrent users across regions, with automated scaling and failover ensuring a seamless experience.

Summary

Auto-scaling and failover patterns are essential to ensure that applications remain available and responsive under all conditions. Azure provides enterprise-grade capabilities for both reactive and proactive scaling, as well as intelligent traffic management for regional resilience.

Key takeaways:

- Use **App Service Autoscale, VMSS**, **AKS HPA**, and **Functions** to scale resources automatically.
- Integrate **Azure Monitor** to trigger scaling actions based on performance metrics.
- Design failover using **Azure Front Door**, **Traffic Manager**, and **geo-redundant services.**
- Combine **Availability Zones, sets**, and **replication** for high availability.
- Continuously test scaling and failover behavior with load simulations and chaos engineering.

The next chapter will explore patterns for building powerful, data-driven applications in Azure using lakes, warehouses, and real-time analytics.

Chapter 8: Design Patterns for Data-Driven Solutions

Data Lake and Big Data Solutions

In the age of digital transformation, organizations are collecting data at an unprecedented rate—from web applications, IoT devices, social media, internal systems, and third-party sources. However, collecting data is only the first step. To extract meaningful insights and drive innovation, businesses need a scalable, secure, and flexible data architecture that supports raw data ingestion, transformation, exploration, and analysis. This is where **data lakes** and **big data solutions** come into play.

Azure offers a powerful ecosystem for building data lakes and managing big data workflows using services like **Azure Data Lake Storage (ADLS)**, **Azure Data Factory**, **Azure Synapse Analytics**, **Azure Databricks**, **Azure Stream Analytics**, and **HDInsight**. This section dives into architecture design patterns, ingestion techniques, transformation pipelines, security strategies, and best practices for building scalable data-driven solutions on Azure.

Data Lake Architecture: Overview

A **data lake** is a centralized repository that allows you to store all structured and unstructured data at any scale. Unlike traditional databases or data warehouses, data lakes store raw data in its native format until needed.

Key Components

- **Ingestion Layer**: Ingests data from various sources (batch and streaming)
- **Storage Layer**: Raw zone, curated zone, and analytics-ready zone
- **Processing Layer**: Data transformation and enrichment
- **Consumption Layer**: BI tools, analytics engines, ML models
- **Governance and Security**: Metadata, access control, and monitoring

---

Choosing Azure Data Lake Storage (ADLS)

ADLS Gen2 is built on top of Azure Blob Storage and adds hierarchical namespace support, fine-grained security, and Hadoop compatibility.

Features

- Unlimited storage
- Scalable throughput
- Native support for directories and files
- POSIX-compliant ACLs
- Azure AD-based authentication

```
az storage account create \
—name mydatalake \
—resource-group myRG \
—sku Standard_LRS \
—kind StorageV2 \
—hierarchical-namespace true
```

Ingesting Data into the Data Lake

Azure supports both **batch** and **streaming** data ingestion.

Batch Ingestion with Azure Data Factory (ADF)

ADF is a cloud-based ETL service that enables data movement and transformation across 90+ sources.

```
{
"name": "CopyPipeline",
"properties": {
"activities": [
{
"name": "CopyFromSQLToADLS",
"type": "Copy",
"inputs": [{ "referenceName": "SQLDataset" }],
"outputs": [{ "referenceName": "ADLSDataset" }]
```

}

]

}

}

Streaming Ingestion with Azure Event Hubs

Stream IoT or event-based data using Azure Event Hubs → Stream Analytics → ADLS.

az eventhubs namespace create—name mynamespace—resource-group myRG—location eastus

az eventhubs eventhub create—name myhub—namespace-name mynamespace—message-retention 1

Data Lake Zones

Divide the data lake into logical zones for better manageability and governance.

Zone	Purpose
Raw Zone	Original data in source format
Curated Zone	Cleaned and transformed data
Gold Zone	Aggregated, analytics-ready datasets

Each zone may be stored in a separate container or directory within ADLS.

Data Transformation Patterns

Use tools like **Azure Data Factory**, **Azure Synapse Pipelines**, or **Azure Databricks** for transformation tasks.

Common Patterns

- Schema on read/write
- Slowly changing dimensions
- Data format conversions (CSV → Parquet)
- Filtering, joins, aggregations

Databricks Example: Convert CSV to Parquet

df = spark.read.csv("abfss://raw@mydatalake.dfs.core.windows.net/sales.csv", header=True)

df.write.parquet("abfss://curated@mydatalake.dfs.core.windows.net/sales_parquet")

Apache Parquet is commonly used for analytical workloads due to its columnar storage and compression efficiency.

Metadata Management and Cataloging

Use **Azure Purview** or **Microsoft Fabric Data Catalog** to manage metadata:

- Discover data assets
- Track lineage
- Apply classifications and sensitivity labels
- Enable data governance

Security in Data Lake Solutions

Security should be enforced at multiple levels:

Identity and Access Management

- Use **Azure AD** for identity-based access control
- Define **POSIX ACLs** for folders and files in ADLS Gen2

az storage fs access set \

—path raw/sales \

—acl "user:john:rw-,group::r—,other::—-" \

—account-name mydatalake

Data Encryption

- Data is encrypted at rest with Microsoft-managed keys or **customer-managed keys** via Azure Key Vault
- TLS 1.2 enforced for in-transit data

Data Lineage and Compliance

Data governance includes tracking how data flows and transforms across systems.

- Capture lineage with **Azure Data Factory** and **Synapse**
- Use **Azure Monitor** and **Log Analytics** to audit data access and job executions

- Integrate **Microsoft Purview** for regulatory compliance (e.g., GDPR, HIPAA)

Consumption and Analytics

After data is prepared, expose it to consumers using:

- **Power BI** for dashboards and reports
- **Synapse SQL Serverless** for ad-hoc queries
- **Databricks** for ML model training
- **Azure ML** for experimentation and deployment

Example: Query Parquet with Synapse Serverless

```
SELECT COUNT(*) FROM OPENROWSET(
BULK 'https://mydatalake.dfs.core.windows.net/curated/sales_parquet/',
FORMAT='PARQUET'
) AS sales;
```

Best Practices

- **Partition data** by time or region for better query performance
- Use **Parquet or Avro** for efficient storage and analytics
- Design pipelines as **idempotent** to support re-runs

- Automate **data quality checks** at every transformation stage
- **Tag** assets with metadata for discoverability

Real-World Scenario: Telecommunications Data Lake

A telecom provider ingests call records, usage logs, and device telemetry:

- **Raw Zone**: Stores daily CSV exports from switches and routers
- **Curated Zone**: Processes and joins data with user profiles using Databricks
- **Gold Zone**: Aggregates subscriber metrics per region for Power BI
- **Azure Event Hubs**: Ingests real-time SMS delivery statuses
- **Azure Data Factory**: Orchestrates hourly and daily batch ETL
- **Azure Purview**: Catalogs all datasets and applies retention policies

The solution supports over 20 TB of ingested data per day and provides real-time insights to network operations and marketing.

Summary

Data lakes empower organizations to manage large, diverse datasets flexibly and cost-effectively. Azure Data Lake and its surrounding ecosystem enable you to build secure, scalable, and intelligent data platforms.

Key takeaways:

- Use **ADLS Gen2** for scalable, secure storage with hierarchical namespace support
- Ingest data using **Data Factory**, **Event Hubs**, and **Stream Analytics**
- Organize data into **raw**, **curated**, and **gold** zones
- Perform transformations using **ADF**, **Databricks**, and **Synapse**
- Govern and secure your data with **Purview**, **ACLs**, and **Key Vault**
- Empower analysts and data scientists with **Power BI**, **Synapse SQL**, and **Azure ML**

The next section explores how to derive real-time value from streaming data using Azure Stream Analytics and event processing pipelines.

Real-Time Analytics with Azure Stream Analytics

As businesses evolve into data-driven organizations, the ability to process and respond to information in real time becomes a competitive advantage. From detecting fraud within milliseconds to monitoring sensor data in manufacturing plants, **real-time analytics** enables organizations to derive insights and trigger actions without delay.

Azure provides a robust, fully managed platform for real-time stream processing through **Azure Stream Analytics (ASA)**. Built for scalability and ease of use, ASA allows developers to query and transform streaming data using SQL-like syntax, integrate with multiple data sources and sinks, and scale with minimal operational overhead.

This section covers architecture design, use cases, stream processing patterns, integrations, and best practices for implementing real-time analytics solutions using Azure Stream Analytics.

The Value of Real-Time Analytics

Traditional batch analytics introduces latency that can be unacceptable in scenarios where data freshness is critical. Real-time analytics enables:

- **Anomaly detection** in security, operations, and transactions
- **Monitoring** of user interactions and system health
- **Automation** of alerts, escalations, and responses
- **Personalization** in e-commerce and media streaming
- **Operational dashboards** with live KPIs

Core Components of Azure Stream Analytics

Azure Stream Analytics enables real-time ingestion, processing, and output of streaming data with minimal setup.

Component	Description
Input	Data streams from Event Hubs, IoT Hub, or Blob Storage
Query	SQL-like language for filtering, aggregation, joining
Output	Azure SQL, Cosmos DB, Power BI, Data Lake, etc.
Job	The end-to-end execution unit of an ASA pipeline

Common Real-Time Analytics Architecture

Example Flow:

1. Devices or applications send data to **Azure Event Hub** or **IoT Hub**.
2. **ASA job** reads from the stream, processes data in real time.
3. Processed results are written to **Power BI**, **Azure SQL**, or **Blob Storage**.

This architecture can also incorporate **Azure Functions** for custom actions or **Logic Apps** for workflow orchestration.

Creating an Azure Stream Analytics Job

```
az stream-analytics job create \

—name RealTimeJob \

—resource-group myRG \

—location eastus \

—output-error-policy Drop \
```

—data-locale "en-US"

Adding an Input (Event Hub)

az stream-analytics input create \

—job-name RealTimeJob \

—name SensorInput \

—type Stream \

—datasource EventHub \

—eventhub-namespace myeventhubns \

—eventhub-name sensordata \

—shared-access-policy-name RootManageSharedAccessKey \

—resource-group myRG

Adding an Output (Blob Storage)

az stream-analytics output create \

—job-name RealTimeJob \

—name BlobOutput \

—datasource Blob \

—storage-account-name mystorage \

—container-name outputcontainer \

—path-pattern "{date}/{time}" \

—resource-group myRG

Writing Stream Queries

Stream Analytics uses a declarative SQL-like language for processing data.

Simple Filtering

```
SELECT * FROM SensorInput

WHERE temperature > 75
```

Aggregation Over Time Window

```
SELECT

deviceId,

AVG(temperature) AS avgTemp

FROM SensorInput

GROUP BY TUMBLINGWINDOW(minute, 1), deviceId
```

Joining Two Streams

```
SELECT

i.deviceId,

i.temperature,

m.maintenanceDate

FROM SensorInput i
```

```
JOIN MaintenanceSchedule m
ON i.deviceId = m.deviceId
AND DATEDIFF(minute, i, m) BETWEEN 0 AND 5
```

Stream Analytics supports **tumbling**, **hopping**, and **sliding** windows for time-based aggregations.

Output Destinations

Stream results can be sent to various destinations for further analysis or reporting.

- **Azure SQL Database**: For live dashboards and alerts
- **Azure Cosmos DB**: For high-speed, schema-less data access
- **Azure Data Lake**: For long-term storage and batch analytics
- **Power BI**: For real-time visualization
- **Azure Functions**: To trigger workflows or alerts

Example: Output to Power BI

```
az stream-analytics output create \
—job-name RealTimeJob \
—name PowerBIOutput \
—datasource PowerBI \
```

```
—dataset-name RealTimeMetrics \
—table-name DeviceStats \
—resource-group myRG
```

Real-Time Alerts and Automation

Combine ASA with Azure Functions or Logic Apps to automatically respond to specific conditions.

Example Use Case

- Detect when humidity exceeds a threshold.
- Trigger an Azure Function that sends a push notification or turns on a cooling system.

```
SELECT
deviceId, humidity
INTO AlertOutput
FROM SensorInput
WHERE humidity > 90
```

Integration with IoT Hub

When working with thousands of devices, use **Azure IoT Hub** as the ingestion point. ASA can ingest directly from IoT Hub's event stream and apply filtering, enrichment, and transformation logic.

Example Scenario

- IoT sensors send temperature and vibration data to IoT Hub
- ASA filters out noise and performs anomaly detection
- Alerts are written to SQL DB and sent to an admin dashboard

---

Monitoring and Scaling ASA Jobs

Azure Monitor integrates with ASA to track:

- Input event counts
- Output write latency
- Function execution time
- Errors and dropped events

Set **alerts** on metrics like LateInputEvents, RuntimeErrors, or BackloggedInputEvents.

Scaling ASA

- Stream Analytics jobs automatically scale to handle throughput up to 200 MB/s per streaming unit.
- Increase **Streaming Units (SUs)** for higher parallelism.

```
az stream-analytics job update \
```

—name RealTimeJob \

—resource-group myRG \

—streaming-units 6

Best Practices

- **Design for idempotency**: Ensure reprocessed events don't corrupt data
- **Use partitioned input sources** for scalability
- **Compress and encode data** (e.g., Avro, JSON) for efficiency
- **Tune time windows** based on data arrival characteristics
- **Apply watermarking** to handle late-arriving events
- Store raw events in **Data Lake** for historical analysis

Real-World Scenario: Smart City Traffic Monitoring

A city-wide traffic system uses Stream Analytics for real-time insights:

- **IoT Edge devices** stream data from traffic cameras and sensors
- ASA processes over 100K events per second for congestion detection

- **Power BI dashboards** show live traffic density by intersection
- Alerts trigger rerouting instructions to digital signage and mobile apps
- All raw data is stored in ADLS for post-event simulation and optimization

This enables responsive traffic management, improved safety, and better city planning.

Summary

Azure Stream Analytics empowers developers to build robust, real-time data pipelines that support dynamic decision-making, operational efficiency, and customer engagement.

Key takeaways:

- Use **ASA** for real-time stream processing with minimal overhead
- Connect to **Event Hubs**, **IoT Hub**, and **Blob Storage** as data sources
- Write rich, SQL-based queries with windowing, joins, and aggregations
- Output to destinations like **Power BI**, **SQL DB**, **Cosmos DB**, or **Functions**
- Monitor jobs and autoscale for high-throughput workloads

- Combine ASA with **Data Lake**, **Logic Apps**, and **Azure ML** for end-to-end analytics

The next section will explore data warehousing patterns using **Azure Synapse Analytics**, unlocking insights through petabyte-scale analytics and integrated SQL and Spark engines.

Data Warehousing Patterns with Synapse Analytics

In the modern data ecosystem, organizations are not only required to store large volumes of data—they must also analyze it efficiently, integrate it with diverse sources, and deliver insights to decision-makers in real-time or near-real-time. Traditional data warehouses were designed for structured data and batch processing, but today's enterprises demand systems that can handle structured, semi-structured, and unstructured data at scale, with high performance and concurrency.

Azure Synapse Analytics (formerly SQL Data Warehouse) is Microsoft's unified data analytics platform that combines **data integration**, **data warehousing**, and **big data analytics** into a single service. It enables seamless querying of data using both **SQL** and **Apache Spark**, and integrates deeply with **Power BI**, **Azure Data Lake**, and **Machine Learning** tools.

This section explores architecture design, data modeling, transformation patterns, performance optimization, and operational best practices for implementing enterprise-grade data warehousing solutions with Azure Synapse Analytics.

Why Azure Synapse Analytics?

Azure Synapse Analytics empowers organizations to:

- Run complex queries over petabytes of data
- Perform on-demand analytics using serverless SQL pools
- Blend structured and unstructured data sources
- Build unified pipelines for data movement and transformation
- Enable self-service analytics for BI teams
- Integrate with modern ML workflows

It offers **both provisioned (dedicated)** and **on-demand (serverless)** query engines, letting you balance cost and performance.

Synapse Components

Component	Description
Dedicated SQL Pool	Massively parallel processing (MPP) data warehouse for high performance
Serverless SQL Pool	Query data in ADLS without pre-provisioning infrastructure
Apache Spark Pool	Perform large-scale analytics using Spark with Synapse Studio
Synapse Studio	Unified UI for data exploration, ingestion, transformation, and visualization

Data Warehousing Architecture with Synapse

A typical Synapse-based data warehouse architecture includes:

1. **Data Ingestion**: From ERP, CRM, IoT, and clickstream

sources via Azure Data Factory or Synapse Pipelines

2. **Staging Area**: Raw data stored in Azure Data Lake
3. **Transformation**: ETL/ELT using SQL scripts or Spark notebooks
4. **Presentation Layer**: Star/snowflake schemas in Synapse tables
5. **Visualization**: Live dashboards in Power BI, integrated with Synapse

---

Creating a Dedicated SQL Pool

```
az synapse workspace create \

—name myworkspace \

—resource-group myRG \

—storage-account mystorage \

—file-system myfilesystem \

—sql-admin-login myadmin \

—sql-admin-password MySecurePassword123

az synapse sql pool create \

—name mydedicatedpool \

—workspace-name myworkspace \

—performance-level DW100c
```

Use the dedicated SQL pool for workloads with predictable usage and complex transformations.

Data Modeling Patterns

Star Schema

- **Fact tables** store metrics (e.g., sales, transactions)
- **Dimension tables** provide context (e.g., product, region, time)

```
CREATE TABLE FactSales (

SaleID INT,

ProductID INT,

RegionID INT,

Quantity INT,

TotalAmount FLOAT,

SaleDate DATE

)

CREATE TABLE DimProduct (

ProductID INT,

ProductName NVARCHAR(100),

Category NVARCHAR(50)

)
```

Snowflake Schema

- Normalized version of the star schema
- Reduces redundancy at the cost of more complex joins

Use star schemas when simplicity and query speed are key; use snowflake schemas when space and consistency are priorities.

Data Loading Patterns

PolyBase for Bulk Loading

PolyBase enables fast parallel ingestion from Blob Storage or ADLS into Synapse.

CREATE EXTERNAL DATA SOURCE MyExternalData

WITH (

TYPE = HADOOP,

LOCATION = 'abfss://raw@mystorage.dfs.core.windows.net/'

);

CREATE EXTERNAL FILE FORMAT MyFileFormat

WITH (

FORMAT_TYPE = DELIMITEDTEXT,

FORMAT_OPTIONS (FIELD_TERMINATOR = ',', STRING_DELIMITER = '"')

);

```
CREATE EXTERNAL TABLE ExternalSales (
SaleID INT, ProductID INT, Amount FLOAT
)
WITH (
LOCATION = 'sales.csv',
DATA_SOURCE = MyExternalData,
FILE_FORMAT = MyFileFormat
);
```

Then insert into internal tables:

```
INSERT INTO FactSales
SELECT * FROM ExternalSales;
```

Querying External Data with Serverless SQL

```
SELECT
customerId,
COUNT(*) AS orderCount
FROM
OPENROWSET(
BULK 'https://mystorage.dfs.core.windows.net/curated/orders/*.parquet',
FORMAT='PARQUET'
```

```
) AS orders

GROUP BY customerId;
```

Serverless SQL is ideal for ad-hoc queries and exploration of data in Data Lake without requiring ETL.

Performance Optimization

Distribution Methods

- **Hash**: Evenly spreads rows using a key (best for large fact tables)
- **Round Robin**: Default; good for staging or small tables
- **Replicate**: Copies data to every node (best for small dimensions)

```
CREATE TABLE FactOrders

WITH

(

DISTRIBUTION = HASH(OrderID),

CLUSTERED COLUMNSTORE INDEX

)

AS SELECT * FROM StagingOrders;
```

Indexing

- Use **Clustered Columnstore Index** for compression and analytics
- Use **Heap** or **Clustered Index** for small lookup tables or transactional tables

---

ETL and ELT Pipelines

Use Synapse Pipelines or Azure Data Factory for orchestration:

- **Copy Activity** to ingest from SQL, Blob, SaaS apps
- **Data Flow** for visual transformations (filter, join, map)
- **Notebook Activity** to invoke Spark transformations
- **Stored Procedure Activity** for pushing down logic into Synapse

---

Integrating with Power BI

- Use **DirectQuery** for real-time dashboards (serverless SQL)
- Use **Import Mode** for high-performance visuals with cached data
- Leverage **Synapse-managed Power BI datasets** for unified modeling

---

Security and Governance

Data Masking

```
CREATE TABLE Employees (
SSN VARCHAR(11) MASKED WITH (FUNCTION = 'partial(0,"XXX-XX-",4)'),
FullName NVARCHAR(100)
)
```

Row-Level Security (RLS)

```
CREATE SECURITY POLICY RegionFilter
ADD FILTER PREDICATE Region = USER_NAME()
ON dbo.Sales;
```

Integration with Purview

Use Microsoft Purview to:

- Discover data assets in Synapse
- Classify sensitive columns (e.g., PII)
- Apply data retention and sharing policies

Real-World Scenario: Retail Demand Forecasting

A global retailer uses Synapse Analytics to:

- Load 20+ years of sales, weather, and promotions data
- Clean and model data using Spark notebooks
- Serve a dimensional model to BI users in Power BI
- Forecast demand using ML models trained in Azure ML
- Refresh dashboards daily using Synapse Pipelines
- Implement RLS to restrict store managers to their regional data

The solution supports 500 concurrent BI users and generates insights across 50,000+ SKUs.

Summary

Azure Synapse Analytics is a powerful platform for building enterprise-grade data warehousing and analytics solutions that unify structured and unstructured data, SQL and Spark, and batch and real-time processing.

Key takeaways:

- Use **dedicated SQL pools** for predictable, high-performance workloads
- Use **serverless SQL** for exploration and ad-hoc analytics
- Apply **star and snowflake schemas** to structure your data warehouse

- Load data efficiently using **PolyBase** and **Data Factory**
- Optimize with **distribution**, **indexes**, and **data compression**
- Secure and govern data with **masking**, **RLS**, and **Purview**
- Enable seamless integration with **Power BI**, **ML**, and **Data Lake**

With these patterns, organizations can unlock the full value of their data and deliver insights at scale across departments and industries. The next chapter explores the principles and implementation of Serverless and Event-Driven Architecture in Azure.

Chapter 9: Serverless and Event-Driven Architecture

Triggers and Bindings in Azure Functions

Serverless computing is transforming the way developers build and run applications by abstracting away infrastructure concerns, enabling rapid deployment, and allowing for auto-scaling with demand. Azure Functions, a core component of Azure's serverless platform, enables developers to execute event-driven code with minimal setup and cost. It eliminates the need to provision and manage servers, allowing teams to focus purely on application logic.

Azure Functions is built on a **trigger and binding** model that simplifies integration with a variety of services. A **trigger** defines how a function is invoked (e.g., via an HTTP request or a message in a queue), while **bindings** connect functions to other services for input or output (e.g., storage blobs, databases, or event streams).

This section explores in-depth how triggers and bindings work in Azure Functions, including configuration, patterns, practical examples, and best practices for building scalable, maintainable event-driven solutions.

Understanding Triggers

A trigger is a declaration of the event that causes a function to execute. Each function must have exactly one trigger.

Supported Trigger Types

- **HTTP Trigger**: Respond to HTTP requests (e.g., REST API endpoints)

- **Timer Trigger**: Execute on a schedule (CRON expressions)
- **Blob Trigger**: React to new or modified blobs in Azure Storage
- **Queue Trigger**: Process messages from Azure Storage queues
- **Service Bus Trigger**: Consume messages from Service Bus queues or topics
- **Event Hub Trigger**: Stream analytics processing
- **Cosmos DB Trigger**: React to changes in a Cosmos DB container
- **SignalR Trigger**: Real-time communications

Example: HTTP-triggered function in C#

```
[FunctionName("HttpExample")]

public static async Task<IActionResult> Run(

[HttpTrigger(AuthorizationLevel.Function, "get", "post", Route = null)] HttpRequest req,

ILogger log)

{

string name = req.Query["name"];

return new OkObjectResult($"Hello, {name}");

}
```

Working with Bindings

Bindings simplify access to external resources. A function can have **zero or more input and output bindings**, which are automatically managed by the runtime.

Binding Direction

- **Input Binding**: Data your function reads from
- **Output Binding**: Where your function writes to

Example: Azure Blob output binding in function.json

```
{
"bindings": [
{
"type": "blob",
"direction": "out",
"name": "outputBlob",
"path": "samples-output/{rand-guid}.txt",
"connection": "AzureWebJobsStorage"
}
]
}
```

Combining Triggers and Bindings

Functions become powerful when you combine triggers and bindings to build full event-driven workflows.

Example: Queue Trigger + Blob Output

```
[FunctionName("QueueToBlob")]

public static void Run(

[QueueTrigger("input-queue", Connection = "AzureWebJobsStorage")] string queueItem,

[Blob("output-container/{rand-guid}.txt", FileAccess.Write)] out string outputBlob,

ILogger log)

{

outputBlob = queueItem.ToUpper();

}
```

This function takes a message from a queue and writes it to a blob.

Timer Trigger

Timer triggers are useful for scheduled tasks like nightly cleanup, periodic notifications, or status updates.

```
[FunctionName("TimerExample")]

public static void Run(

[TimerTrigger("0 */5 * * * *")] TimerInfo myTimer,
```

```
ILogger log)
{
log.LogInformation($"Timer triggered at: {DateTime.Now}");
}
```

The expression "0 */5 * * * *" runs the function every 5 minutes.

Input Bindings Examples

Cosmos DB Input

```
[FunctionName("ReadFromCosmos")]
public static IActionResult Run(
[HttpTrigger(AuthorizationLevel.Function, "get", Route = null)] HttpRequest req,
[CosmosDB(
databaseName: "ProductsDB",
collectionName: "Products",
ConnectionStringSetting = "CosmosDBConnection",
SqlQuery = "SELECT * FROM Products p WHERE p.category = 'electronics'")] IEnumerable<dynamic> products,
ILogger log)
{
return new OkObjectResult(products);
```

```
}
```

Output Bindings Examples

Service Bus Output

```
[FunctionName("WriteToServiceBus")]
public static void Run(
[HttpTrigger(AuthorizationLevel.Function, "post", Route = null)] HttpRequest req,
[ServiceBus("mytopic", Connection = "ServiceBusConnection")] out string message,
ILogger log)
{
message = "New message from Function App";
}
```

Advanced Binding Scenarios

Multiple Bindings

Functions can interact with multiple services simultaneously.

```
[FunctionName("FanOutProcessor")]
public static void Run(
[QueueTrigger("input-queue")] string input,
```

```
[CosmosDB("LogsDB", "Audit", ConnectionStringSetting = "CosmosDBConnection")] out dynamic document,

[ServiceBus("alerts", Connection = "ServiceBusConnection")] out string alert)

{

document = new { id = Guid.NewGuid(), message = input, timestamp = DateTime.UtcNow };

alert = $"Processed message: {input}";

}
```

Configuration and Deployment

Bindings and triggers are configured via:

- **Attributes** in C# code
- **function.json** in JavaScript/Python

Use **local.settings.json** for local development connection strings.

```
{

"IsEncrypted": false,

"Values": {

"AzureWebJobsStorage": "UseDevelopmentStorage=true",

"FUNCTIONS_WORKER_RUNTIME": "dotnet"

}

}
```

Deployment can be automated using:

- Azure CLI (az functionapp deployment)
- GitHub Actions
- Azure DevOps Pipelines
- ARM/Bicep/Terraform for infrastructure

Monitoring and Diagnostics

Azure Functions integrates with:

- **Application Insights**: Logs, metrics, failures
- **Live Metrics Stream**: Real-time observability
- **Log Analytics**: KQL-based querying

KQL Example:

```
requests

| where cloud_RoleName == "MyFunctionApp"

| summarize count() by resultCode, bin(timestamp, 5m)
```

Set alerts on execution failures or long durations to maintain reliability.

Best Practices

- Keep functions **stateless** for maximum scalability
- **Use bindings over SDKs** to simplify code

- Apply **retry policies** on triggers like Queue and Service Bus
- Use **dead-letter queues** to handle poison messages
- Organize code in **separate functions per responsibility**
- Store secrets in **Azure Key Vault**, not environment variables

---

Real-World Scenario: Order Processing Pipeline

An e-commerce company implements an order processing system using Azure Functions:

- **HTTP Trigger** receives new orders from the website
- **Queue Output Binding** pushes order IDs to a processing queue
- **Queue Trigger Function** validates inventory, updates SQL DB
- **Blob Binding** stores invoice PDF
- **Service Bus Binding** sends a confirmation email via third-party service
- **Timer Trigger** runs every night to archive logs to Azure Data Lake

This architecture scales to handle peak traffic during promotions and integrates seamlessly with internal systems and SaaS APIs.

Summary

Azure Functions' triggers and bindings model provides a powerful, declarative way to integrate serverless logic with the Azure ecosystem. By reacting to events and binding seamlessly to data sources, you can create highly scalable, maintainable, and testable workflows without complex boilerplate.

Key takeaways:

- Triggers define **when** a function runs; bindings define **what it connects to**
- Azure Functions support a wide array of triggers including **HTTP**, **Timer**, **Queue**, **Blob**, and **Event Hub**
- Use input/output bindings to avoid manual SDK integrations
- Monitor function health and performance with **Application Insights**
- Build clean, decoupled, event-driven workflows with **minimum infrastructure**

The next section will focus on **Durable Entities and State Management**, enabling long-running, stateful workflows within a serverless context using Durable Functions.

Durable Entities and State Management

Serverless computing shines in event-driven, stateless scenarios. However, many real-world applications require **stateful** behavior—retaining data across function executions, coordinating long-running operations, managing timeouts, and tracking workflows. In traditional systems, state is typically stored in databases or caches. In Azure Functions, the **Durable Functions** extension introduces a powerful pattern for managing stateful operations without managing infrastructure.

Durable Functions enable **orchestration**, **stateful entities**, and **long-running workflows** using reliable checkpoints, input/output bindings, and a robust task framework. Among its features, **Durable Entities** provide a scalable abstraction for modeling individual units of state with simple and familiar syntax.

This section explores how to use Durable Entities in Azure Functions for advanced state management scenarios. We'll cover design principles, coding patterns, real-world examples, scaling considerations, and integration with event sources and outputs.

What Are Durable Entities?

A **Durable Entity** is a lightweight serverless object that maintains its own state across invocations. Each entity is identified by an **Entity ID** (name + key) and is automatically persisted by the Durable Functions runtime.

Durable Entities:

- React to **operations**, such as Add, Update, or Reset
- Store state automatically and durably
- Support **multi-entity coordination**
- Scale elastically with Azure Functions infrastructure

Entities behave like **actors**—they encapsulate state and behavior, and messages (operations) are dispatched to them for processing.

When to Use Durable Entities

Durable Entities are ideal for:

- **Shopping cart/session management** in e-commerce
- **IoT device state tracking**
- **User profile or preference management**
- **Inventory or stock control**
- **Workflow step tracking**
- **Per-customer limits, counters, and quotas**

Unlike orchestrator functions, which model workflows, entities model stateful *objects.*

Anatomy of a Durable Entity Function

A Durable Entity function is a special Azure Function with the [FunctionName] and [EntityTrigger] attributes.

Example in C#:

```
[JsonObject(MemberSerialization.OptIn)]

public class Counter

{

[JsonProperty("value")]

public int Value { get; set; }

public void Add(int amount) => Value += amount;
```

```
public void Reset() => Value = 0;

public int Get() => Value;

[FunctionName("Counter")]

public static Task Run([EntityTrigger] IDurableEntityContext ctx)

=> ctx.DispatchAsync<Counter>();

}
```

This entity holds an integer and supports three operations: Add, Reset, and Get.

Interacting with Durable Entities

You interact with Durable Entities using a **client function**, which may be an HTTP trigger, timer, queue trigger, or another orchestrator.

Send Operations

```
[FunctionName("IncrementCounter")]

public static async Task<IActionResult> Run(

[HttpTrigger(AuthorizationLevel.Function, "post", Route = "increment/{id}")] HttpRequest req,

[DurableClient] IDurableEntityClient client,

string id)

{

EntityId entityId = new EntityId("Counter", id);
```

```
await client.SignalEntityAsync(entityId, "Add", 1);
return new OkResult();
}
```

Read State

```
[FunctionName("ReadCounter")]
public static async Task<IActionResult> Run(
[HttpTrigger(AuthorizationLevel.Function, "get", Route = "counter/{id}")] HttpRequest req,
[DurableClient] IDurableEntityClient client,
string id)
{
EntityId entityId = new EntityId("Counter", id);
var stateResponse = await client.ReadEntityStateAsync<Counter>(entityId);
return stateResponse.EntityExists
? new OkObjectResult(stateResponse.EntityState.Value)
: new NotFoundResult();
}
```

Lifecycle of a Durable Entity

1. **Created** when first signaled or explicitly instantiated

2. **Active** while handling operations
3. **Idle** after execution completes (state is persisted)
4. **Deleted** when removed via DeleteEntityAsync

Entity state is stored in Azure Storage Table behind the scenes, ensuring durability and high availability.

Durable Entities vs Durable Orchestrations

Feature	Durable Entities	Durable Orchestrations
Purpose	Stateful objects with encapsulated logic	Long-running workflows
State Model	Object state (class)	Workflow state (steps and history)
Scalability	Massive horizontal scale	Suitable for fewer, complex flows
Communication	Via signals	Via method calls and tasks
Use Case Examples	Shopping cart, counters	Approval workflows, timers, chaining

Use orchestrations for **business process flows**, and entities for **stateful logic per ID/key.**

State Management Patterns

Counters and Aggregates

Entity per key (e.g., product ID), updating counts in response to events.

Timers and Expiry

Use orchestrator or timer-triggered functions to signal expiration operations on entities.

Event Sourcing

Instead of directly modifying state, store event logs in a blob, and replay events to rebuild state.

Durable Entity Signals from Events

You can integrate Durable Entities with other Azure services:

- **Event Hub**: Process event stream and update device/ entity state
- **Service Bus**: Handle messages for specific entity IDs
- **Blob Trigger**: Signal entities to process newly uploaded files

Example: Signal from Service Bus Trigger

```
[FunctionName("ProcessDeviceCommand")]

public static async Task Run(

[ServiceBusTrigger("device-events")] string message,

[DurableClient] IDurableEntityClient client)

{

var data = JsonConvert.DeserializeObject<DeviceCommand>(message);
```

```
var entityId = new EntityId("DeviceState", data.DeviceId);

await client.SignalEntityAsync(entityId, data.Command, data.Payload);

}
```

Best Practices

- **Use batching** for high-throughput scenarios
- **Avoid large state**—limit state size to <64 KB for performance
- **Design idempotent operations** to tolerate retries
- **Implement versioning** when changing entity logic
- **Clean up** unused entities to reduce storage overhead
- **Monitor** with Application Insights and Log Analytics

Monitoring Durable Entities

Use built-in logging and metrics:

- Operation latency
- Failed executions
- Storage usage
- Entity count over time

KQL Example for failed entity executions:

```
traces
| where customDimensions["FunctionName"] == "Counter"
| where severityLevel == 3
| project timestamp, message
```

Real-World Scenario: IoT Device State Tracking

A logistics company manages thousands of delivery trucks with IoT sensors. Each truck has:

- **Entity ID** = Truck ID
- **State** = location, fuel level, status
- Event Hub streams telemetry into Azure
- Service Bus relays commands (e.g., reroute, pause)
- Durable Entities store state per truck and update as messages arrive
- Periodic aggregations are run by orchestrator functions

This solution ensures real-time visibility of every vehicle with minimal infrastructure overhead and high reliability.

Summary

Durable Entities provide a scalable, fault-tolerant, and code-centric way to model stateful objects in serverless applications. By leveraging the event-driven model and built-in persistence of Azure Functions, developers can build sophisticated, stateful systems that scale with demand and stay responsive to events.

Key takeaways:

- Use Durable Entities to manage **per-entity state**, such as counters, profiles, or device status
- Model behavior using **operations**, and retain state between executions automatically
- Integrate with **HTTP**, **Service Bus**, **Event Hub**, or **Timers** for signals
- Monitor and scale entity workloads with **Application Insights** and **Durable Task Hub**
- Prefer entities over orchestrations when modeling **lightweight, reactive, parallelizable** logic

The next section explores **Logic Apps for Workflow Orchestration**, focusing on low-code event-driven workflows that integrate with hundreds of services across Azure and beyond.

Logic Apps for Workflow Orchestration

Workflow automation is essential in modern cloud architectures. It enables organizations to connect systems, integrate services, automate repetitive tasks, and ensure consistent processes across applications. Azure Logic Apps is a serverless workflow automation engine designed to orchestrate tasks and business processes across both cloud and on-premises systems using a visual designer and a large catalog of connectors.

Logic Apps allows developers and IT professionals to define workflows declaratively, using a graphical interface or JSON code. It supports a wide range of triggers and actions, including HTTP requests, scheduled intervals, and events from Azure services or external SaaS systems.

In this section, we will explore the structure of Logic Apps, common patterns, integration scenarios, control flow mechanisms, monitoring, and best practices for building resilient, scalable workflows.

Core Concepts of Logic Apps

Logic Apps enable **workflow orchestration** using a series of steps called **actions**, triggered by an initial **event**. Each Logic App is composed of:

- **Triggers** – Define the event that initiates the workflow
- **Actions** – Define what the workflow does (e.g., call an API, send email)
- **Connectors** – Provide integration with services like Outlook, SQL Server, Blob Storage, etc.
- **Control Flow** – Enables conditional logic, loops, scopes, parallelism

Logic Apps are ideal for:

- Data ingestion and transformation
- Automated approval processes
- Notifications and alerting
- B2B integration (EDI, AS2)

- Long-running business workflows

Creating a Logic App

Logic Apps can be created through:

- Azure Portal (Visual Designer)
- Visual Studio Code (Logic Apps Standard)
- ARM/Bicep templates or Terraform
- REST API or Azure CLI

```
�az logic workflow create \
—resource-group myRG \
—name OrderWorkflow \
—definition @workflow.json \
—location eastus
�
```

Trigger Types

Logic Apps support many trigger types:

- **Recurrence** – Run at specific intervals
- **HTTP** – Trigger on incoming requests
- **Event Grid/Event Hub/Service Bus** – Trigger on messages or events

- **SaaS Triggers** – E.g., "When an email arrives" (Outlook)

Example: Recurrence trigger (every 5 minutes)

```
◈{
"type": "Recurrence",
"recurrence": {
"frequency": "Minute",
"interval": 5
}
}
◈
```

Actions and Connectors

Logic Apps include 500+ connectors. Examples:

- **Azure Blob Storage** – Read/write files
- **Office 365 Outlook** – Send/receive email
- **Azure SQL Database** – Insert or query data
- **ServiceNow** – Create tickets
- **Twilio** – Send SMS
- **Custom APIs** – via HTTP action or custom connector

Example: Send email action

```
{
"type": "ApiConnection",
"inputs": {
"host": {
"connection": {
"name": "@parameters('$connections')['office365']['connectionId']"
}
},
"method": "post",
"path": "/v2/Mail"
}
}
```

Control Flow and Logic

Logic Apps support:

- **Conditions (if/else)**
- **Switch statements**
- **For-each loops**
- **Until loops**

- **Scopes** (try/catch/finally equivalent)
- **Parallel branches**

Example: Condition check

```
{
"condition": "@equals(triggerBody()['status'], 'approved')",
"actions": {
"SendApprovedEmail": {
"type": "ApiConnection",
"inputs": { /* email details */ }
}
}
}
```

Using Variables and Expressions

Logic Apps support variables, expressions, and built-in functions for transformations.

Declare and set variables:

```
{
"type": "InitializeVariable",
"inputs": {
```

"name": "Total",

"type": "int",

"value": 0

}

}

�Use expressions:

�"@add(variables('Total'), 10)"

�

Advanced Patterns

Long-Running Workflows

- Logic Apps support **stateful execution** with automatic checkpointing
- Use **Delay**, **Until**, and **Scope** actions for waiting and retries

Human Interaction Workflows

- Integrate with **Approvals in Teams or Outlook**
- Wait for responses before proceeding

Event-Driven Automation

- Triggered by **Azure Event Grid**, **Blob creation**, or **Service Bus message**
- Useful for infrastructure automation, alert processing, etc.

Integration with External Systems

Logic Apps can connect to virtually any external system using:

- **Built-in connectors**
- **HTTP/REST APIs**
- **On-premises Data Gateway** for SQL Server, SAP, file shares
- **Custom connectors** with OpenAPI or Postman collections

Example: HTTP action to invoke external API

```
{
"type": "Http",
"inputs": {
"method": "POST",
"uri": "https://api.contoso.com/invoice",
"body": {
```

```
"amount": "@triggerBody()['amount']"
}
}
}
```

Error Handling and Resiliency

Logic Apps have built-in retry and error handling:

- **Automatic retries** for transient errors
- **Scopes** can be used to catch and handle failures
- **Configure run-after** settings to define fallback logic
- Send alerts or logs on failure

```
"runAfter": {
"PreviousAction": [
"Failed"
]
}
```

Monitoring and Diagnostics

Monitoring tools:

- **Run history**: View each workflow execution and step details
- **Azure Monitor**: Collect telemetry, set alerts
- **Log Analytics**: Query logs with KQL
- **Application Insights**: Optional integration for advanced telemetry

Example KQL query:

```
AzureDiagnostics
| where ResourceType == "WORKFLOWS"
| summarize count() by Status_s, bin(TimeGenerated, 1h)
```

CI/CD for Logic Apps

Use **ARM templates**, **Bicep**, or **Terraform** for infrastructure as code. Combine with **Azure DevOps** or **GitHub Actions** for deployment automation.

Example GitHub Action:

```
- name: Deploy Logic App
uses: Azure/arm-deploy@v1
with:
resourceGroupName: myRG
template: ./logicapp.bicep
```

Real-World Scenario: Invoice Processing Workflow

A financial services company uses Logic Apps to automate invoice workflows:

1. **Trigger**: Invoice PDF uploaded to Blob Storage
2. **Extract metadata** with Azure Form Recognizer (via REST API)
3. **Condition**: Validate vendor ID and total
4. **Insert** into Azure SQL Database
5. **Notify** finance team via Outlook
6. **Create task** in Planner or send to ERP system

This results in 70% reduction in manual effort and near real-time processing of inbound invoices.

Best Practices

- Use **resource naming conventions** for Logic Apps and connectors
- Keep workflows **modular**—use nested Logic Apps or child workflows
- Avoid large payloads—prefer references (e.g., blob URLs) to data
- **Log custom telemetry** for business traceability
- Use **stateful mode** for long workflows and **stateless mode** for API-style flows

Summary

Azure Logic Apps enable the creation of powerful, scalable, and maintainable workflows with minimal code. By connecting services and automating business processes, organizations can improve efficiency, reduce errors, and enhance responsiveness.

Key takeaways:

- Logic Apps support **event-driven**, **timer-based**, and **manual** triggers
- Use **connectors** to integrate with hundreds of Azure and third-party services
- Employ **conditions, loops, scopes**, and **parallelism** for control flow
- Handle **errors gracefully** using retry policies and fallback paths
- Monitor workflows using **Azure Monitor**, **Log Analytics**, and **run history**
- Automate deployment with **CI/CD pipelines**

With Logic Apps, developers and business users alike can orchestrate processes that span the cloud and enterprise systems, transforming manual tasks into efficient automated workflows. The next chapter will showcase real-world case studies that apply these patterns in production environments.

Chapter 10: Case Studies and Real-World Applications

Migrating Monolith to Microservices in Azure

Many organizations face the challenge of modernizing legacy applications. These applications, often built using monolithic architectures, tend to suffer from scalability bottlenecks, deployment delays, tight coupling, and limited maintainability. Migrating such systems to a cloud-native microservices architecture on Azure can deliver transformative benefits—agility, independent scalability, faster releases, and improved fault isolation.

This case study walks through the strategic, architectural, and technical steps involved in migrating a legacy monolithic application to a microservices-based solution using Azure services. It presents real-world lessons learned, tools used, and patterns applied during the migration journey.

Legacy System Overview

The subject of this case study is a 12-year-old enterprise resource planning (ERP) application used by a mid-sized manufacturing company. The application was built using .NET Framework 4.6, deployed on Windows servers, and backed by a single SQL Server database. Key characteristics included:

- Monolithic codebase (600k+ lines of code)
- Tight coupling between modules (inventory, finance, orders, reports)

- Weekly manual deployments with significant downtime
- Performance bottlenecks under concurrent loads
- Difficult integration with modern APIs and external systems

---

Migration Objectives

The business stakeholders outlined the following goals for the modernization effort:

1. **Improve system scalability** to handle seasonal spikes
2. **Enable continuous deployment** with minimal risk
3. **Modularize the application** to enable team autonomy
4. **Integrate easily** with third-party and cloud services
5. **Optimize cost and operational efficiency**

To meet these objectives, the team chose a **microservices architecture** deployed in Azure, gradually refactoring and rehosting individual components.

Target Architecture in Azure

The future-state architecture was designed with cloud-native principles:

- **Azure Kubernetes Service (AKS)** to host containerized microservices
- **Azure API Management** as the unified entry point and gateway

- **Azure SQL and Cosmos DB** for data storage (based on workload needs)
- **Azure Key Vault** for secrets and credentials
- **Azure Monitor** and **Application Insights** for observability
- **Azure DevOps** for CI/CD and IaC pipelines
- **Event-driven patterns** using Azure Event Grid and Service Bus

Each domain (e.g., orders, finance, inventory) became a separate microservice with its own data store and API contract.

Step 1: Assessment and Decomposition

The first step involved understanding the monolith's structure, dependencies, and usage patterns.

Tools and techniques used:

- **Dependency mapping tools** (e.g., NDepend, Structure101)
- **Code metrics and hotspots** (cyclomatic complexity, change frequency)
- **Business capability mapping** (bounded contexts for DDD)

Modules were prioritized based on:

- Business criticality

- Change frequency
- Integration complexity
- Team readiness

The **Order Management** module was chosen as the first candidate for extraction.

Step 2: Strangling the Monolith

The **Strangler Fig Pattern** was used to incrementally replace parts of the monolith without disrupting the entire system.

1. A façade layer was introduced using **Azure API Management**
2. New requests were routed to microservices while legacy endpoints were proxied
3. Each new microservice was deployed to **AKS** with its own CI/CD pipeline
4. A **shared message bus** (Azure Service Bus) coordinated async events
5. The monolith continued to serve unported modules behind the façade

This pattern allowed for **coexistence** and **gradual migration**, reducing risk.

Step 3: Building Microservices

Microservices were built using:

- **.NET 6 in Docker containers**

- REST APIs with **OpenAPI definitions**
- **EF Core** or **Dapper** for database access
- **Azure SQL** for transactional services
- **Cosmos DB** for high-scale, distributed reads (e.g., product catalog)

Each service adhered to **12-factor principles**, including:

- Independent deployments
- Stateless containers
- Externalized config (from Key Vault)
- Health checks and logging

Example Dockerfile:

```
FROM mcr.microsoft.com/dotnet/aspnet:6.0 AS base

WORKDIR /app

COPY . .

ENTRYPOINT ["dotnet", "OrderService.dll"]
```

Step 4: Data Strategy

Data was decoupled using **database per service** and **eventual consistency** patterns.

- Services owned their own schemas

- **Change Data Capture (CDC)** was used to sync from the monolith temporarily
- **Outbox pattern** ensured reliable event publishing
- **CQRS** and **Event Sourcing** were applied selectively (e.g., order tracking)

Read models were exposed via **GraphQL API** or API composition layers.

Step 5: Observability and Resilience

A key goal was to ensure visibility across the distributed system.

Implemented:

- **Structured logging** with Serilog to Azure Monitor
- **Distributed tracing** with Application Insights (custom telemetry IDs)
- **Retry and Circuit Breaker patterns** using Polly
- **Health checks** exposed on /healthz endpoints
- **Kubernetes probes** for liveness and readiness

KQL sample to trace API errors:

```
traces
| where message contains "OrderService"
| where severityLevel >= 3
| summarize count() by operation_Name, resultCode
```

Step 6: CI/CD and Infrastructure as Code

CI/CD pipelines were built using **Azure DevOps**:

- **Build**: Dockerize and scan images
- **Release**: Helm deploy to AKS via YAML pipelines
- **Secrets** pulled from Key Vault using managed identities
- **Terraform** or **Bicep** templates for repeatable infra provisioning

Example Bicep snippet:

```
resource aks 'Microsoft.ContainerService/managedClusters@2021-03-01' = {
name: 'erp-aks'
location: resourceGroup().location
properties: {
agentPoolProfiles: [
{
name: 'agentpool'
count: 3
vmSize: 'Standard_DS2_v2'
}
]
```

```
}
}
```

Step 7: Training and Change Management

To support the transition:

- Developers were trained in **Kubernetes**, **containerization**, and **DDD**
- Monitoring dashboards were created in **Grafana** and **Power BI**
- Business users were onboarded to API-based interfaces
- Feature toggles allowed controlled rollouts

The team used **feature flags** to route subsets of traffic to new services and rolled back easily if needed.

Results and Outcomes

Within nine months:

- Over 60% of the monolith was replaced by independently deployed microservices
- Release cycles improved from **weekly** to **daily**
- Outages dropped by 75% thanks to fault isolation and retries
- Time to onboard new features decreased by 40%

- Integration with external systems improved through well-defined APIs

The remaining modules were scheduled for phased migration, using lessons from early iterations.

Summary

Migrating a monolithic application to microservices on Azure requires careful planning, stakeholder alignment, technical excellence, and incremental delivery. By applying proven patterns such as the Strangler Fig, Domain-Driven Design, and containerization, organizations can modernize their systems while minimizing disruption.

Key takeaways:

- Use **API Management** and **Service Bus** to bridge old and new systems
- Apply **Strangler Pattern** for safe incremental migration
- Favor **database-per-service** and **event-driven** communication
- Use **AKS**, **Key Vault**, and **Application Insights** for scalable, secure operations
- Empower teams with **automation**, **observability**, and **autonomy**

The next section explores a FinTech application that embraces event-driven architecture in Azure from day one, illustrating how to architect greenfield systems with flexibility and performance in mind.

A FinTech Application Using Event-Driven Design

The financial technology (FinTech) sector demands rapid innovation, regulatory compliance, and the ability to scale securely in response to customer needs and market volatility. This case study examines the design and implementation of a greenfield FinTech application built from the ground up using an **event-driven architecture** on Azure. The goal was to leverage serverless computing, microservices, and cloud-native patterns to deliver a scalable, resilient, and flexible financial services platform.

The application, called **NeoBank**, is a digital-only banking solution offering services such as current accounts, payments, savings, and financial insights. From onboarding to real-time transaction notifications, every feature in NeoBank is powered by events flowing through a reactive, distributed system.

Objectives and Requirements

The design team defined the following goals for NeoBank:

1. **Asynchronous communication** to decouple services and reduce latency
2. **Elastic scalability** with cost-efficient infrastructure
3. **Secure data handling** in compliance with PCI DSS and GDPR
4. **High availability and resilience**
5. **Real-time processing** for payments, fraud detection, and notifications
6. **Auditability and traceability** for all system events

With these in mind, the architecture was built using **Azure-native services**, emphasizing **event-driven patterns** and **serverless infrastructure**.

Core Architecture Overview

NeoBank's architecture follows an **event-driven microservices** model, centered around Azure Event Grid and Azure Service Bus. Major components include:

- **Azure API Management (APIM)** for exposing secure, versioned APIs
- **Azure Functions** for stateless compute
- **Azure Event Grid** for domain events and event subscriptions
- **Azure Service Bus** for command handling and message queuing
- **Azure Cosmos DB** for high-velocity, low-latency transactional data
- **Azure Blob Storage** for document and file storage (e.g., KYC documents)
- **Azure Key Vault** for managing secrets, certificates, and encryption keys
- **Azure Monitor** and **Application Insights** for observability
- **Azure Static Web Apps** hosting React-based frontend for clients

Domain-Driven Microservices

The application was decomposed into domain-focused services aligned with **Bounded Contexts**:

Microservice	Responsibility
Identity Service	User registration, authentication (OAuth2)
Account Service	Manages accounts, balances, statements
Payments Service	Handles transfers, bill payments
Fraud Service	Detects suspicious activity in real-time
Notifications	Sends SMS, push, and email alerts
Insights Service	Aggregates spending and saving patterns

Each service emitted domain events (e.g., AccountCreated, PaymentInitiated, FraudDetected) to the Event Grid.

Event Flow Example: Payment Initiation

1. The user submits a transfer request via the mobile app
2. API Gateway routes to a **PaymentInitiationFunction**
3. The function validates the request and sends a PaymentInitiated event to Event Grid
4. **Fraud Service** and **Notification Service** are subscribed to this event
5. Fraud checks are performed; if clear, the **FundsTransferFunction** executes
6. The **Account Service** updates balances and emits PaymentCompleted
7. The **Notification Service** sends a push notification to the user

This decoupled, event-driven approach ensures services can evolve independently and scale based on their own workloads.

Azure Functions Implementation

Each domain service exposes multiple Azure Functions, grouped by domain logic.

Example: Payment Initiation Function

```
[FunctionName("PaymentInitiationFunction")]

public static async Task<IActionResult> Run(

[HttpTrigger(AuthorizationLevel.Function, "post", Route = "payments/initiate")] HttpRequest req,

[EventGrid(TopicEndpointUri = "PaymentEvents", TopicKeySetting = "EventGridKey")] IAsyncCollector<EventGridEvent> outputEvents,

ILogger log)

{

var payment = JsonConvert.DeserializeObject<Payment>(await new StreamReader(req.Body).ReadToEndAsync());

var evt = new EventGridEvent(

subject: $"payments/{payment.Id}",

eventType: "PaymentInitiated",

data: payment,

dataVersion: "1.0");

await outputEvents.AddAsync(evt);
```

```
return new OkObjectResult(new { status = "submitted" });
}
```

Event Grid Subscriptions

Each microservice subscribes to relevant events via Event Grid.

- **Push-based** delivery
- Supports retry policies and dead-lettering
- Subscriptions are filtered by event type and subject

```
az eventgrid event-subscription create \
—name FraudCheckerSub \
—source-resource-id /subscriptions/.../topics/PaymentEvents \
—endpoint https://fraudservice.azurewebsites.net/runtime/webhooks/EventGrid?functionName=CheckPayment \
—included-event-types PaymentInitiated
```

Message Bus for Commands

While Event Grid handles events, **Azure Service Bus** is used for commands that require guaranteed delivery and ordering, such as:

- DebitAccountCommand
- InitiateSettlementCommand

Services process messages via **queue-triggered functions**, ensuring at-least-once delivery and dead-lettering on failure.

Observability and Auditing

Observability is critical in FinTech. NeoBank uses:

- **Application Insights** for telemetry (requests, dependencies, traces)
- **Azure Monitor Alerts** for failures, performance thresholds
- **Log Analytics** with KQL for diagnostics

```
customEvents
| where name == "PaymentInitiated"
| summarize count() by tostring(customDimensions.accountId), bin(timestamp, 5m)
```

Event sourcing is used for audit logs—every domain event is stored immutably in Azure Blob Storage and optionally indexed in Cosmos DB.

Security and Compliance

Security is paramount:

- **Azure AD B2C** provides secure OAuth2/OIDC login for users
- **Key Vault** stores API keys, client secrets, and certificates
- All APIs are protected behind **Azure API Management** with rate limiting and IP filtering

- **Encryption at rest** and **in transit** is enforced for all services
- **GDPR-compliant deletion** patterns are implemented (e.g., Data Erasure Event)

CI/CD and Infrastructure Automation

CI/CD pipelines were built with **GitHub Actions**:

- Build/test/deploy functions and frontend
- Validate infrastructure templates (Bicep)
- Publish events for deployment status tracking

Example deployment workflow:

```
jobs:
deploy:
runs-on: ubuntu-latest
steps:
- name: Deploy Functions
uses: Azure/functions-action@v1
with:
app-name: payments-fn
package: './PaymentsFunction'
```

Infrastructure is managed via Bicep:

```
resource eventGrid 'Microsoft.EventGrid/topics@2021-06-01-preview' = {
name: 'PaymentEvents'
location: resourceGroup().location
sku: {
name: 'Basic'
}
properties: {
inputSchema: 'EventGridSchema'
}
}
```

Results and Business Impact

Within 6 months of launch:

- System handled over **250K transactions/month**
- Average API response times: **<200ms**
- Fraud detection latency reduced to **<1 second**
- 99.99% uptime with zero major outages
- Customer support tickets related to delays dropped by 60%

- Dev teams released new features weekly with full rollback capability

The event-driven model proved ideal for a financial app requiring modularity, responsiveness, and security.

Summary

This case study demonstrates how Azure's event-driven services can be combined to build powerful, scalable FinTech applications. With Event Grid, Service Bus, Functions, and Cosmos DB, developers can create a distributed system that's fast, reliable, and maintainable.

Key takeaways:

- Use **Event Grid** for decoupled, fan-out event publishing
- Use **Service Bus** for guaranteed command processing
- Build scalable, testable logic in **Azure Functions**
- Implement **observability**, **auditing**, and **compliance** from day one
- Automate deployment with **CI/CD pipelines** and **Bicep/ARM**

In the next section, we'll explore how an e-commerce platform built a high-throughput, API-driven backend on Azure to serve global traffic with elasticity and reliability.

E-commerce Platform with Scalable APIs

In a digital-first world, e-commerce businesses are expected to deliver fast, reliable, and personalized experiences to a global customer base. Downtime, latency, or a poor user experience can directly translate to lost revenue. This case study examines the architectural evolution of a large online retail platform as it migrated to **Azure-native, API-first, scalable microservices** to meet increasing customer demand, seasonal traffic spikes, and global reach expectations.

The platform, known as **RetailNow**, initially began as a monolithic ASP.NET MVC application hosted on on-premises infrastructure. Over the course of a year, it transitioned to a fully containerized microservices ecosystem on Azure Kubernetes Service (AKS), integrated with Azure API Management and a suite of data and messaging services for elasticity and availability.

Business Drivers

RetailNow's leadership team initiated the modernization effort with the following objectives:

1. **Elastic Scalability**: Handle Black Friday and promotional surges without pre-provisioning excess resources
2. **Global Reach**: Deliver low-latency experiences in North America, Europe, and Asia
3. **API-first Platform**: Enable third-party integrations, mobile apps, and in-store kiosks through a consistent API layer
4. **Rapid Releases**: Shorten feature delivery cycles and roll back safely when needed
5. **High Availability**: Eliminate single points of failure and

maintain uptime even during infrastructure outages

Architecture Overview

The target architecture leveraged core Azure services to meet these goals:

- **Azure API Management** (APIM) to centralize and secure access to all APIs
- **Azure Kubernetes Service (AKS)** for deploying containerized services with auto-scaling
- **Azure Cosmos DB** and **Azure SQL Database** for polyglot persistence
- **Azure Redis Cache** for session and catalog caching
- **Azure Event Grid** and **Service Bus** for event-driven integration
- **Azure Front Door** and **Traffic Manager** for global traffic routing and failover
- **Azure Monitor**, **Application Insights**, and **Log Analytics** for observability

Each business domain—such as Catalog, Cart, Checkout, Payments, and User—was deployed as an independent microservice.

API Strategy with APIM

RetailNow adopted an **API-first development strategy**, with APIM serving as the central entry point for:

- Public partner APIs (e.g., order tracking, product availability)
- Internal APIs (e.g., pricing, inventory)
- Mobile and frontend clients (e.g., React SPA, mobile apps)

APIM provided:

- **Rate limiting** and **IP filtering**
- **Subscription keys** and **OAuth 2.0** validation
- **API versioning**
- **Analytics and diagnostics**

Example: Policy to limit traffic to 100 requests per minute per user

```
<rate-limit-by-key calls="100" renewal-period="60" counter-key="@(context.Request.Headers.GetValueOrDefault("x-user-id", "anonymous"))" />
```

Stateless Services on AKS

Microservices were containerized using Docker and deployed to AKS with **Helm charts** and **Horizontal Pod Autoscaler** (HPA).

Service example: Product Catalog

- Stateless .NET 6 API
- Read-heavy workload (over 2M requests/day)

- Backed by Cosmos DB for high-speed, globally distributed reads
- Redis used for caching top products and recent views

Kubernetes HPA definition:

```
apiVersion: autoscaling/v2

kind: HorizontalPodAutoscaler

metadata:

name: catalog-hpa

spec:

scaleTargetRef:

apiVersion: apps/v1

kind: Deployment

name: catalog-api

minReplicas: 2

maxReplicas: 20

metrics:

- type: Resource

resource:

name: cpu

target:
```

type: Utilization

averageUtilization: 70

Event-Driven Order Processing

The Checkout service emits a OrderPlaced event to Azure Event Grid, triggering downstream services asynchronously:

1. **Inventory Service** reserves stock
2. **Payment Service** captures funds and issues receipts
3. **Shipping Service** schedules logistics
4. **Notification Service** sends SMS and email
5. **Analytics Service** logs data to Data Lake for dashboards

This pattern improves responsiveness and allows services to scale independently.

Data Strategy

The platform implemented a **polyglot persistence** model:

- **Cosmos DB** for catalog and user profiles
- **Azure SQL** for transactional order processing
- **Blob Storage** for media assets (images, videos)
- **Redis** for volatile session and cart data

Caching patterns reduced load on the database:

```
public async Task<Product> GetProduct(string id)

{
```

```
var cached = await _cache.GetStringAsync(id);

if (cached != null) return JsonConvert.DeserializeObject<Product>(cached);

var product = await _cosmosDb.GetProductAsync(id);

await _cache.SetStringAsync(id, JsonConvert.SerializeObject(product), new DistributedCacheEntryOptions

{

AbsoluteExpirationRelativeToNow = TimeSpan.FromMinutes(10)

});

return product;

}
```

Security and Compliance

RetailNow enforced secure API consumption through:

- **OAuth 2.0 / OpenID Connect** via Azure AD B2C for customer authentication
- **Managed identities** for service-to-service access to Key Vault and databases
- **Data encryption** at rest and in transit using Azure default encryption
- **WAF** via Azure Front Door to prevent injection attacks and enforce request schemas

- **Compliance checks** for PCI DSS and GDPR, including data retention and access logging

---

Monitoring and Observability

The observability stack included:

- **Application Insights** for per-service telemetry and tracing
- **Log Analytics** for querying logs across all microservices
- **Prometheus + Grafana** (via AKS add-ons) for container metrics
- **Alerts** on 5xx error spikes, slow endpoints, and failed transactions

KQL query example for top slow APIs:

```
requests
| where duration > 3000
| summarize avg(duration), count() by name
| top 5 by avg_duration desc
```

CI/CD and DevOps

Each microservice had its own CI/CD pipeline using Azure DevOps:

- **Build** Docker image

- **Scan** for vulnerabilities (e.g., Trivy)
- **Push** to Azure Container Registry
- **Deploy** to AKS with Helm or Kustomize
- **Rollback** on failure with Helm revision history

Infrastructure-as-Code was implemented with **Bicep**:

```
resource apim 'Microsoft.ApiManagement/service@2021-08-01' = {
name: 'retail-apim'
location: 'eastus'
sku: {
name: 'Developer'
capacity: 1
}
properties: {
publisherEmail: 'devops@retailnow.com'
publisherName: 'RetailNow'
}
}
```

Business Impact

Within one year of migration:

- Peak traffic support increased by 400%
- Average page load time dropped by 42%
- Checkout abandonment rate decreased by 17%
- Platform availability maintained at 99.99%
- Time-to-market for new features improved from bi-monthly to weekly releases

The system supported over **10 million monthly users** across three continents with full failover and scaling capabilities.

Summary

RetailNow's journey illustrates how modern e-commerce platforms can harness Azure's scalable and serverless services to deliver robust, performant, and customer-centric digital experiences. The combination of API-first strategy, microservices, event-driven communication, and strong DevOps practices ensured that the platform could innovate rapidly while maintaining enterprise-grade reliability.

Key takeaways:

- Use **APIM** for API governance, security, and lifecycle management
- Deploy microservices on **AKS** with **auto-scaling** and **observability**
- Apply **event-driven architecture** for decoupled, responsive systems

- Leverage **polyglot persistence** with Cosmos DB, SQL, and Redis
- Automate everything with **CI/CD pipelines** and **IaC**

With these practices in place, RetailNow continues to grow and evolve, delivering a resilient, global commerce experience to millions of customers.

Chapter 11: Appendices

Glossary of Terms

The world of Azure cloud architecture and design patterns involves a vast array of terminologies, abbreviations, and conceptual jargon. To ensure readers have a comprehensive understanding of the material covered throughout this book, this section provides a glossary of key terms used across cloud-native architectures, Azure services, serverless computing, and DevOps pipelines.

This glossary serves as a quick reference and is especially useful when dealing with cross-disciplinary teams where engineers, architects, DevOps professionals, and business stakeholders may interpret technical terms differently. The terms are listed alphabetically for ease of navigation.

A

API (Application Programming Interface)

A contract or set of rules that allow software applications to communicate with each other. APIs are central to microservices, integrations, and serverless architectures.

API Gateway

A service that sits between clients and backend services, routing requests, enforcing policies, aggregating responses, and enabling observability. Azure API Management (APIM) is Azure's API gateway solution.

AKS (Azure Kubernetes Service)

A managed Kubernetes platform that simplifies the deployment, management, and operations of containerized applications in Azure.

B

Blob Storage

A scalable object storage solution by Azure for storing large amounts of unstructured data such as documents, images, videos, and logs.

Bicep

A domain-specific language (DSL) for declaratively deploying Azure resources, offering a cleaner syntax than traditional ARM JSON templates.

C

CDN (Content Delivery Network)

A globally distributed network that caches content closer to users to reduce latency. Azure CDN is integrated with services like Blob Storage and Front Door.

CI/CD (Continuous Integration / Continuous Deployment)

A development practice that automates the building, testing, and deployment of code changes to deliver updates faster and more reliably.

Cosmos DB

Azure's globally distributed, multi-model NoSQL database service optimized for low-latency and high-throughput applications.

CQRS (Command Query Responsibility Segregation)

A design pattern that separates read and write operations into different models to improve scalability, maintainability, and performance.

D

Durable Functions

An extension of Azure Functions that enables the creation of stateful workflows and orchestrations using function chaining, fan-out/fan-in, and entities.

DevOps

A cultural and technical movement aimed at unifying development and operations teams through automation, monitoring, and continuous delivery.

DNS (Domain Name System)

A naming system that maps human-readable domain names to IP addresses. Azure DNS is used to manage DNS zones in the cloud.

E

Event Grid

An eventing backbone in Azure for building reactive, event-driven architectures. It connects sources (like Blob Storage) to handlers (like Functions).

Elasticity

The ability of a system to automatically scale resources up or down based on load. Azure App Services and AKS support elastic scaling.

F

Function App

An Azure resource that hosts one or more serverless Azure Functions, each triggered by various sources like HTTP, queues, or timers.

Front Door

A scalable entry point for web applications that provides load balancing, SSL offloading, and global routing for high availability and low latency.

G

GitHub Actions

A CI/CD platform integrated with GitHub repositories to automate build, test, and deployment workflows.

Gateway Pattern

An architectural pattern used to encapsulate internal services behind a single entry point, often enforced with policy and security.

H

Horizontal Scaling

Adding more instances of a service to handle increased load. In Azure, services like AKS and App Services support horizontal scaling.

Hybrid Cloud

A computing environment that combines on-premises data centers with public cloud services to achieve flexibility and control.

I

IaC (Infrastructure as Code)

The process of managing and provisioning infrastructure through code rather than manual processes. Supported in Azure via ARM, Bicep, or Terraform.

Identity Provider (IdP)

A system that authenticates user identities and issues security tokens. Azure Active Directory (AD) and Azure AD B2C are examples.

J

JSON (JavaScript Object Notation)

A lightweight data-interchange format used widely in APIs, configuration files, and data serialization in Azure services.

K

Kubernetes

An open-source system for automating deployment, scaling, and operations of application containers. AKS provides Kubernetes as a managed service.

Key Vault

A secure store for secrets, keys, and certificates used by applications. It enables encryption, access control, and auditing.

L

Load Balancer

A device or service that distributes incoming network traffic across multiple backend servers to ensure availability and responsiveness.

Logic Apps

Azure's low-code/no-code workflow automation platform for integrating services and automating business processes across cloud and on-premises.

M

Managed Identity

A feature of Azure Active Directory that allows Azure services to authenticate to each other securely without managing credentials.

Microservices

An architectural style that structures an application as a collection of small, autonomous services modeled around business domains.

N

Network Security Group (NSG)

Azure's firewall-like security construct for controlling inbound and outbound traffic to resources in a virtual network.

O

Observability

The capability of understanding the internal state of a system through its outputs, including logs, metrics, and traces. Azure Monitor provides a unified observability platform.

OpenAPI

A specification for defining REST APIs, formerly known as Swagger. Supported natively in Azure API Management.

P

PaaS (Platform as a Service)

A cloud service model that provides a platform for building and deploying applications without managing underlying infrastructure.

Policy

Rules defined to enforce governance and compliance in cloud environments. Azure Policy helps enforce resource tagging, location restrictions, etc.

Q

Queue Storage

An Azure storage service for storing large numbers of messages, often used for decoupling and asynchronous processing in microservices.

R

Resource Group

A container in Azure for managing and grouping related resources. All Azure resources must reside within a resource group.

Resiliency

The ability of a system to recover from failures and continue to function. Azure services support resiliency through redundancy and failover.

S

Service Bus

A reliable message broker for enterprise integration patterns like pub/sub, FIFO, and message queuing. Supports transactions and dead-lettering.

Serverless

A cloud computing execution model where the cloud provider dynamically manages the infrastructure. Azure Functions and Logic Apps are serverless services.

SLA (Service Level Agreement)

A contractual commitment between a provider and user that defines availability, performance, and support expectations.

T

Terraform

An open-source infrastructure as code tool used to provision and manage cloud resources across multiple providers, including Azure.

Traffic Manager

An Azure DNS-based traffic load balancer that enables global distribution and failover for services hosted in multiple regions.

U

Uptime

A measure of system availability. Azure provides SLAs that guarantee uptime for various services.

V

Virtual Network (VNet)

A private, logically isolated section of the Azure cloud where resources can securely communicate.

Virtual Machine (VM)

An emulation of a physical computer hosted in Azure. VMs offer full control over OS and software configuration.

W

Web App

A PaaS offering in Azure for hosting websites, RESTful APIs, and backend services with auto-scaling, patching, and CI/CD support.

Webhook

A method for augmenting or altering the behavior of a web application with custom callbacks, triggered by events.

Summary

This glossary captures the essential terms and concepts used throughout the book and in real-world Azure cloud architecture. By referencing this section, readers can bridge knowledge gaps, clarify ambiguous terms, and enhance communication across development, architecture, operations, and business teams.

Whether you're architecting cloud-native solutions, writing Terraform, or deploying microservices to AKS, understanding these terms is foundational to success in the Azure ecosystem.

Resources for Further Learning

Cloud architecture is a constantly evolving discipline that spans multiple domains—compute, storage, networking, security, DevOps, data, AI, and more. To stay current and deepen your expertise, it's essential to continually engage with educational materials, documentation, best practice guides, certifications, open-source tools, and communities.

This section offers a curated list of resources across various formats to help you advance your learning in Azure and cloud-native development. These resources span beginner to expert level and cover theoretical understanding, practical implementation, architecture strategy, and continuous professional growth.

Official Microsoft Azure Documentation

The official Microsoft Azure documentation is the most authoritative and regularly updated source for understanding services, configurations, APIs, and usage patterns.

- **Azure Documentation Home**:

  https://learn.microsoft.com/en-us/azure/

- **Azure Architecture Center**:

  https://learn.microsoft.com/en-us/azure/architecture/

- **Azure Patterns and Practices**:

  https://learn.microsoft.com/en-us/azure/architecture/patterns/

- **Azure Reference Architectures**:

  https://learn.microsoft.com/en-us/azure/architecture/reference-architectures/

These pages offer conceptual overviews, implementation steps, deployment templates, and decision guidance.

Learning Platforms and Tutorials

Microsoft Learn

Microsoft Learn is a gamified, self-paced training platform offering interactive labs and real-world use cases.

- **Start learning Azure**:

  https://learn.microsoft.com/en-us/training/paths/azure-fundamentals/

Key learning paths:

- Azure Fundamentals
- Azure Developer Associate
- Azure Solutions Architect Expert
- DevOps Engineer Expert

Pluralsight

Pluralsight offers in-depth video courses taught by Azure MVPs and architects.

Recommended authors:

- **Scott Allen**
- **Troy Hunt**
- **Tim Warner**
- **Orin Thomas**

LinkedIn Learning

Business-focused tutorials on cloud architecture, DevOps, and Azure certifications.

Books and Publications

Some of the most respected titles in the Azure ecosystem include:

- **"Microsoft Azure Architect Technologies Exam Ref AZ-305"** – by Mike Pfeiffer and Derek Schauland

  Ideal for preparing for certification while learning real-world architecture practices.

- **"Azure for Architects"** – by Ritesh Modi

  Covers cloud design patterns, DevOps, microservices, and hybrid cloud scenarios.

- **"The Phoenix Project"** – by Gene Kim, Kevin Behr, and George Spafford

Not Azure-specific, but highly relevant to understanding DevOps transformation.

- **"Cloud Design Patterns" (Microsoft)** –

A freely available ebook from Microsoft that introduces cloud-centric architectural patterns.

https://learn.microsoft.com/en-us/azure/architecture/patterns/

Certifications

Azure certifications validate your skills and knowledge and are recognized industry-wide. Microsoft offers role-based certifications tailored to job roles:

1. **AZ-900: Azure Fundamentals**
2. **AZ-104: Azure Administrator**
3. **AZ-204: Azure Developer**
4. **AZ-305: Azure Solutions Architect Expert**
5. **AZ-400: Azure DevOps Engineer Expert**
6. **SC-300: Microsoft Identity and Access Administrator**
7. **DP-203: Data Engineering on Microsoft Azure**

Certification paths are detailed here:

https://learn.microsoft.com/en-us/certifications/

Community and Open Source

GitHub

Microsoft maintains a wealth of open-source repositories, samples, and SDKs.

Top repos to explore:

- https://github.com/Azure/azure-quickstart-templates

  1000+ deployable templates using ARM and Bicep

- https://github.com/Azure/azure-sdk-for-net

  SDKs for .NET developers building on Azure

- https://github.com/microsoft/Enterprise-Scale

  A reference implementation for building enterprise-scale landing zones

Tech Community

- **Microsoft Tech Community (Azure)**:

  https://techcommunity.microsoft.com/t5/azure/ct-p/Azure

  Features product announcements, discussions, blogs, and webinars.

- **Stack Overflow Azure Tag**:

  https://stackoverflow.com/questions/tagged/azure

Community support for troubleshooting, best practices, and real-world issues.

Blogs and Podcasts

- **Azure Friday (video series)** – Hosted by Scott Hanselman

  https://azure.microsoft.com/en-us/resources/videos/azure-friday/

- **Microsoft Cloud Show** – Hosted by Andrew Connell and Chris Johnson

  https://www.microsoftcloudshow.com/

- **CloudSkills.fm** – DevOps and cloud engineering with guest experts

  https://cloudskills.io/

- **The Azure Podcast** – Weekly Azure news and interviews

  http://azpodcast.azurewebsites.net/

Developer Tools

Azure provides a range of tools for developers and architects:

- **Azure CLI**

  Cross-platform command line tool:

  https://learn.microsoft.com/en-us/cli/azure/

- **Azure Bicep**

Infrastructure-as-Code DSL:

https://learn.microsoft.com/en-us/azure/azure-resource-manager/bicep/

- **Azure Resource Graph Explorer**

Query Azure resources at scale:

https://portal.azure.com/#blade/HubsExtension/ArgQueryBlade

- **VS Code Extensions for Azure**

https://marketplace.visualstudio.com/items?itemName=ms-vscode.azure-account

---

Architecture Tooling

Visual tools and references:

- **Azure Diagrams Toolkit for Visio**

Download:https://learn.microsoft.com/en-us/azure/architecture/icons/

- **Draw.io / Lucidchart Templates for Azure**

Community-maintained libraries available via their respective marketplaces

- **Azure Well-Architected Framework**

Principles and best practices aligned with performance, cost, security, and operations

https://learn.microsoft.com/en-us/azure/well-architected/

Real-World References

Microsoft Customer Stories

Explore how real companies build on Azure:

- https://customers.microsoft.com/en-us/story/all-stories/

Featured use cases:

- Healthcare compliance with Azure API Management
- Retail scale-out with AKS and Cosmos DB
- Banking innovation with Logic Apps and Functions

Azure Architecture Center Case Studies

- https://learn.microsoft.com/en-us/azure/architecture/example-scenario/

Examples include:

- Scalable web applications
- Secure hybrid networking

- Real-time analytics with Azure Synapse and Stream Analytics

---

Summary

Learning never stops in cloud computing. Azure's ecosystem offers deep technical documentation, hands-on learning platforms, real-world case studies, and an active global community. Whether you're preparing for a certification, designing a new architecture, or troubleshooting an existing system, there are abundant resources available to support you.

Best next steps:

1. Bookmark Microsoft Learn and the Azure Architecture Center
2. Join the Tech Community and GitHub repositories
3. Set a monthly goal for completing a certification or learning path
4. Subscribe to Azure Friday or The Azure Podcast
5. Start contributing to open-source templates or forums

The knowledge you gain today will compound your effectiveness in every future Azure project. Keep building, learning, and sharing.

Sample Projects and Code Snippets

One of the most effective ways to internalize cloud architecture and Azure design patterns is through practical, hands-on projects. In this section, we present a collection of sample projects and code snippets that demonstrate how to implement the key patterns, practices, and services discussed throughout this book. These examples cover a wide range of Azure services and architectural principles, from microservices and serverless workflows to security, monitoring, and DevOps automation.

The following projects are structured for hands-on experimentation, team learning, and prototyping real-world solutions. You are encouraged to clone, modify, and deploy them in your own Azure environments to deepen your practical understanding.

Project 1: Microservices on Azure Kubernetes Service (AKS)

Objective: Build a simple e-commerce backend using microservices for catalog, cart, and checkout domains, deployed to Azure Kubernetes Service.

Technologies Used:

- AKS
- Azure Container Registry (ACR)
- Azure SQL
- Azure Redis
- Azure API Management

Key Patterns Demonstrated:

- API Gateway pattern
- Containerized microservices
- Database-per-service
- Cache-aside pattern

Sample Directory Structure:

```
/ecommerce-aks/
├── catalog-service/
├── cart-service/
├── checkout-service/
├── helm-charts/
├── scripts/
└── k8s-manifests/
```

Catalog Service Dockerfile:

```
FROM mcr.microsoft.com/dotnet/aspnet:6.0
COPY . /app
WORKDIR /app
ENTRYPOINT ["dotnet", "CatalogService.dll"]
```

Helm Values Snippet:

```
replicaCount: 3
image:
repository: myacr.azurecr.io/catalog-service
tag: latest
resources:
limits:
```

```
cpu: 500m
memory: 512Mi
```

Project 2: Serverless Order Workflow with Azure Functions

Objective: Implement a serverless order workflow that processes orders, sends notifications, and logs events.

Technologies Used:

- Azure Functions
- Azure Blob Storage
- Azure Queue Storage
- Azure Table Storage
- Azure Event Grid

Key Patterns Demonstrated:

- Event-driven processing
- Fan-out/fan-in orchestration
- Retry and error handling
- Externalized configuration

Function Trigger Example:

```
[FunctionName("ProcessOrder")]
public static async Task Run(
```

```
[QueueTrigger("orders")] string orderMessage,
[Blob("invoices/{rand-guid}.json", FileAccess.Write)] Stream invoiceOutput,
ILogger log)
{
var invoice = GenerateInvoice(orderMessage);
var json = JsonConvert.SerializeObject(invoice);
using var writer = new StreamWriter(invoiceOutput);
await writer.WriteAsync(json);
}
```

Local.settings.json:

```
{
"IsEncrypted": false,
"Values": {
"AzureWebJobsStorage": "UseDevelopmentStorage=true",
"FUNCTIONS_WORKER_RUNTIME": "dotnet"
}
}
```

Project 3: Real-Time Analytics with Azure Stream Analytics

Objective: Process clickstream data from a website and store aggregated analytics in Azure SQL and Cosmos DB.

Technologies Used:

- Azure Event Hub
- Azure Stream Analytics
- Azure SQL Database
- Azure Cosmos DB
- Azure Data Lake (optional for raw archive)

Stream Analytics Query:

```
SELECT
userId,
COUNT(*) AS PageViews,
System.Timestamp AS AggregatedAt
INTO
SqlOutput
FROM
EventHubInput TIMESTAMP BY EnqueuedTime
GROUP BY
```

TumblingWindow(minute, 5), userId

Deployment Tips:

- Define inputs/outputs in the Stream Analytics job
- Use Data Lake Gen2 for cold path storage
- Monitor job health and configure alerts on watermark delays

---

Project 4: Secure API with Azure API Management and OAuth2

Objective: Create a secure API gateway with API Management, Azure AD B2C, and backends hosted on App Services.

Technologies Used:

- Azure API Management
- Azure AD B2C
- Azure App Service (backend)
- Azure Key Vault

Key Features Demonstrated:

- OAuth2 protection
- Subscription keys
- Custom policies

- Rate limiting

API Management Policy Snippet:

```
<inbound>

<base />

<validate-jwt header-name="Authorization" failed-validation-httpcode="401" require-scheme="Bearer">

<openid-config url="https://login.microsoftonline.com/{tenant}/v2.0/.well-known/openid-configuration" />

<audiences>

<audience>api://my-api</audience>

</audiences>

</validate-jwt>

</inbound>
```

Project 5: Bicep-Based Infrastructure Deployment

Objective: Deploy a full environment using Bicep templates, including a VNet, AKS, Key Vault, and Azure SQL.

Technologies Used:

- Azure Bicep
- Azure CLI
- Azure DevOps or GitHub Actions

Bicep Example:

```
resource sqlServer 'Microsoft.Sql/servers@2022-02-01-preview' = {
name: 'my-sqlserver'
location: resourceGroup().location
properties: {
administratorLogin: 'sqladmin'
administratorLoginPassword: 'secureP@ssw0rd'
}
sku: {
name: 'S0'
tier: 'Standard'
capacity: 10
}
}
```

Pipeline Example (Azure DevOps YAML):

```
trigger:
- main
jobs:
- job: deploy
steps:
```

```
- task: AzureCLI@2
inputs:
azureSubscription: 'MyServiceConnection'
scriptType: 'bash'
scriptLocation: 'inlineScript'
inlineScript: |
az bicep build—file ./main.bicep
az deployment group create \
—resource-group my-rg \
—template-file ./main.json \
—parameters @params.json
```

Project 6: Logic Apps Integration Workflow

Objective: Automate invoice approvals using Logic Apps, Outlook, SharePoint, and SQL Server.

Technologies Used:

- Azure Logic Apps
- Office 365 Outlook
- SharePoint Online
- Azure SQL

Logic App Flow:

1. Trigger: When a file is added to SharePoint
2. Extract invoice metadata
3. Send approval email to manager
4. Insert invoice data into Azure SQL on approval
5. Notify team via Teams

Sample SQL Insert Action:

```
{
"inputs": {
"host": {
"connection": {
"name": "@parameters('$connections')['sql']['connectionId']"
}
},
"method": "post",
"path": "/v2/executeSqlQuery",
"body": {
"query": "INSERT INTO Invoices (InvoiceId, Vendor, Amount) VALUES (@{triggerBody()?['InvoiceId']}, @{triggerBody()?['Vendor']}, @{triggerBody()?['Amount']})"
}
}
}
```

Summary

These sample projects and code snippets offer practical, deployable templates that demonstrate how to build robust, cloud-native applications and infrastructure on Microsoft Azure. By adapting these projects to your use cases, you gain:

- Hands-on experience with Azure services
- Exposure to key design patterns in real-world scenarios
- Confidence in orchestrating microservices, serverless components, and secure APIs
- Insight into modern DevOps pipelines and infrastructure as code

Suggested next steps:

- Fork and clone the repositories on GitHub or Azure DevOps
- Customize for your team's naming conventions, environments, and use cases
- Use these templates for internal learning sessions, demos, or hackathons
- Turn working prototypes into production-ready solutions with monitoring and security hardening

Continue exploring, experimenting, and building. The best way to master cloud architecture is by creating, deploying, and iterating on real systems.

API Reference Guide

As applications evolve to leverage microservices, event-driven logic, and integrations across various services, having a consistent and structured API design becomes critical. APIs serve as the interface between components, users, and services—making them the most exposed and widely consumed part of your architecture. This section provides an in-depth API reference guide based on the architecture patterns and implementations discussed throughout this book.

We'll cover design standards, endpoint conventions, authentication mechanisms, versioning strategies, error handling formats, and documentation approaches that are recommended for Azure-based APIs. The reference includes practical examples using RESTful APIs deployed via Azure API Management, Azure Functions, App Services, and containerized microservices.

API Design Best Practices

Well-designed APIs are predictable, secure, consistent, and self-descriptive. When designing APIs in a cloud-native environment:

1. **Use resource-based URIs**: /products, /orders, /users

2. **Prefer plural nouns**: /items instead of /item

3. **Use HTTP methods correctly**:

○ GET: retrieve resources

○ POST: create resources

○ PUT: update or replace resources

- PATCH: modify resources partially
- DELETE: remove resources

4. **Support filtering, sorting, and pagination** via query parameters
5. **Return appropriate HTTP status codes**
6. **Document with OpenAPI/Swagger**

REST Endpoint Convention Example

Base URL: https://api.retailnow.com/v1

Products API

GET /products # List products

GET /products/{id} # Get product details

POST /products # Create new product

PUT /products/{id} # Update product

DELETE /products/{id} # Delete product

Orders API

GET /orders # List orders

GET /orders/{id} # Order details

POST /orders # Submit a new order

PATCH /orders/{id} # Update status

DELETE /orders/{id} # Cancel order

Common Query Parameters

- ?filter=price gt 100
- ?sort=createdAt desc
- ?page=2&pageSize=20

Request & Response Structure

Request Example (POST Order)

```
{
"userId": "abc123",
"items": [
{ "productId": "p001", "quantity": 2 },
{ "productId": "p002", "quantity": 1 }
],
"shippingAddress": {
"line1": "123 Main St",
"city": "London",
"postcode": "EC1A 1BB"
```

```
}
}
```

Response Example (201 Created)

```
{
"orderId": "ord789",
"status": "Processing",
"estimatedDelivery": "2025-04-27T00:00:00Z"
}
```

Authentication and Authorization

Azure offers multiple options for securing APIs:

OAuth2 + OpenID Connect

- **Azure AD** for internal APIs
- **Azure AD B2C** for external APIs

JWT tokens are passed in Authorization: Bearer {token} headers. Validate using middleware or API Management policy.

Example Policy in Azure API Management

```
<inbound>
<validate-jwt header-name="Authorization" require-scheme="Bearer">
```

```
<openid-config
url="https://login.microsoftonline.com/{tenant-id}/v2.0/.well-known/
openid-configuration" />

<audiences>

<audience>api://my-api-client-id</audience>

</audiences>

</validate-jwt>

</inbound>
```

Versioning Strategy

API versioning ensures backward compatibility as you iterate.

Options:

- **URI versioning (recommended)**: /v1/products
- **Query string**: /products?api-version=1.0
- **Header versioning**: X-API-Version: 1.0

Each version should be:

- Independently deployable
- Well documented
- With deprecation lifecycle

Standard HTTP Status Codes

Status Code	Description
200 OK	Successful request
201 Created	Resource created
204 No Content	Resource deleted
400 Bad Request	Invalid request
401 Unauthorized	Missing or invalid token
403 Forbidden	Authenticated but denied
404 Not Found	Resource does not exist
409 Conflict	Resource already exists
500 Internal Server Error	Server error

Error Handling Format

Use a consistent error response schema:

```
{
"error": {
"code": "InvalidInput",
"message": "Product ID is required.",
"target": "productId",
"details": [
{
"code": "NullValue",
"message": "The productId field cannot be null."
}
```

```
]
}
}
```

Pagination Format

Standard pattern:

- Query params: ?page=1&pageSize=20
- Response:

```
{
"data": [/* items */],
"pagination": {
"page": 1,
"pageSize": 20,
"totalPages": 5,
"totalItems": 100
}
}
```

Rate Limiting

Handled via Azure API Management policies:

```
<rate-limit-by-key calls="1000" renewal-period="3600" counter-key="@(context.Subscription.Id)" />
```

Headers included in response:

- X-RateLimit-Limit
- X-RateLimit-Remaining
- Retry-After

API Documentation with Swagger / OpenAPI

Use the OpenAPI Specification (OAS) for clear and machine-readable API documentation.

Example annotation (ASP.NET Core):

```
/// <summary>Gets a list of all products.</summary>

/// <returns>Product list</returns>

/// <response code="200">Success</response>

[HttpGet]

[ProducesResponseType(StatusCodes.Status200OK)]

public IActionResult GetAllProducts() { ... }
```

Generate Swagger UI via Swashbuckle:

```
dotnet add package Swashbuckle.AspNetCore
```

Serve interactive docs at /swagger/index.html.

Real-World API Design Tips

Use correlation IDs for traceability:

X-Correlation-ID: f2d3a91e-41a3-4e52-9b78-9be52dfae7ad

1.

Implement caching via headers:

Cache-Control: public, max-age=600

2.

Include HATEOAS links for discoverability:

"_links": {

"self": { "href": "/orders/123" },

"cancel": { "href": "/orders/123/cancel" }

}

3.

4. **Design for idempotency** (especially for POST and DELETE)

   ○ Use Idempotency-Key header

API Management Gateway as a Front Door

Azure API Management enables:

- **Centralized control** over APIs
- **Monetization** via developer portals
- **Policy injection** without backend changes

- **Global distribution** with internal/external access

Use APIM to secure backend Functions, App Services, and AKS services. Enable diagnostics and enforce governance.

Summary

APIs are the backbone of any cloud-native application architecture. Whether exposing microservices, orchestrating workflows, or integrating partners, your APIs must be secure, well-documented, versioned, and monitored.

Key takeaways:

- Use resource-oriented URIs and correct HTTP verbs
- Standardize error, pagination, and metadata formats
- Secure APIs with OAuth2 and validate JWTs in API Management
- Version APIs using URI-based strategy and deprecate responsibly
- Automate documentation with OpenAPI and serve Swagger UI
- Leverage Azure API Management for full lifecycle governance

This reference should serve as a blueprint for designing consistent, scalable APIs that integrate cleanly with services across the Azure ecosystem and beyond.

Frequently Asked Questions

This section addresses common questions raised by architects, developers, DevOps engineers, and IT decision-makers as they design, build, and operate Azure-based solutions. Drawing from real-world projects, consulting engagements, and community forums, the FAQs are structured to align with key topics discussed in this book: architecture, scalability, security, cost, serverless, DevOps, and data.

Whether you're just getting started or managing enterprise-grade deployments, these answers are intended to provide clarity and guidance for both strategy and implementation.

Architecture and Design

Q: Should I use microservices for every application?

A: No. Microservices offer modularity, autonomy, and scalability, but they also introduce complexity—especially around service coordination, deployment, observability, and testing. For smaller teams or less complex domains, a well-designed monolith or modular monolith may be more appropriate. Start with a modular architecture and evolve to microservices when bounded contexts are well-understood and the need for independent scaling or deployment becomes clear.

Q: What is the recommended approach for API gateway in Azure?

A: Azure API Management (APIM) is the recommended service for managing APIs. It enables versioning, rate limiting, security enforcement (OAuth2, subscription keys), and logging. For lightweight scenarios or internal services, Azure Application Gateway or even Azure Front Door with routing rules may suffice.

Q: How do I structure my resource groups?

A: Use resource groups to group logically related resources that share the same lifecycle (e.g., an app and its database). Consider structuring by environment (dev, test, prod) and workload (app, data, monitoring). Use naming conventions to support automation and tagging for cost tracking.

Scalability and Performance

Q: What are the best practices for auto-scaling in Azure?

A: Use metrics-based scaling for compute workloads:

- App Services: scale on CPU/memory/requests
- AKS: use HPA and Cluster Autoscaler
- Azure Functions: scale automatically with demand

Use **Azure Monitor autoscale rules** to trigger based on custom metrics. Also, implement **caching**, **async processing**, and **throttling** to reduce load on core systems.

Q: Can I achieve high availability in a single Azure region?

A: Yes, using availability zones (AZs) within a region can offer redundancy. For example:

- AKS can be deployed across AZs
- Azure SQL has zone-redundant offerings

- Load Balancer and Front Door can distribute traffic within zones

For **mission-critical workloads**, deploy to **multiple regions** with Azure Traffic Manager or Front Door to handle failover.

Security and Compliance

Q: What are the top security practices I should follow?

A:

1. **Use managed identities** for service authentication
2. Store secrets in **Azure Key Vault**, not in code or config
3. Enforce **least privilege access** via RBAC
4. Use **NSGs and ASGs** to restrict traffic
5. Enable **Diagnostic Logs**, **Azure Defender**, and **Sentinel**
6. Ensure **encryption at rest and in transit**
7. Review **Azure Security Benchmark** and **Well-Architected Framework**

Q: How do I manage secrets securely in CI/CD pipelines?

A: Store secrets in **Azure Key Vault** and integrate with:

- Azure DevOps using linked service connections

- GitHub Actions via OIDC and federated credentials Never store secrets in code or pipeline YAML files. Use variable groups and secure pipelines with **approval gates** and **auditing.**

Q: How can I ensure GDPR or HIPAA compliance in Azure?

A: Use built-in tools like:

- **Compliance Manager** to map controls
- **Customer Lockbox**, **Information Protection**, and **DLP**
- Configure **data residency** and **data retention policies** Enable **audit logging**, encryption with customer-managed keys, and perform **data discovery** using Azure Purview or Microsoft Priva.

Serverless and Event-Driven

Q: When should I use Azure Functions vs Logic Apps?

A:

- Use **Azure Functions** for code-heavy, event-driven tasks (e.g., image processing, API endpoints)
- Use **Logic Apps** for workflow orchestration and integrations (e.g., approvals, document routing) Both can be combined—e.g., Logic App triggers a Function for transformation.

Q: How do I handle state in serverless applications?

A: Use **Durable Functions** for orchestrations and stateful entities. For other scenarios:

- Use **Azure Table or Cosmos DB** for session state

- Use **Redis** for ephemeral state (e.g., shopping cart) Avoid storing state inside functions directly—functions should be stateless and idempotent.

DevOps and Deployment

Q: What's the best way to manage infrastructure as code in Azure?

A:

- Use **Bicep** for native, modern ARM templates
- Use **Terraform** for multi-cloud or advanced use cases
- Use **GitHub Actions** or **Azure DevOps** for CI/CD
- Keep infrastructure code in version-controlled repos
- Use environments, naming conventions, and tagging standards

---

Q: How do I do blue-green or canary deployments in Azure?

A: Strategies include:

- **App Services**: deployment slots + traffic routing
- **AKS**: use service mesh (e.g., Open Service Mesh) or ingress controllers with traffic splits
- **Functions**: slots + swap or traffic percentages in APIM

These techniques minimize downtime and allow rollback if issues are detected.

Data and Integration

Q: When should I use Cosmos DB vs Azure SQL?

A:

- Use **Cosmos DB** for high-throughput, low-latency, globally distributed apps (NoSQL)
- Use **Azure SQL** for relational workloads with complex joins, ACID transactions, and reporting

If the system mixes read-heavy and transaction-heavy loads, consider **polyglot persistence**—using both as needed.

Q: How can I build real-time analytics pipelines?

A: Use:

- **Azure Event Hub** or **IoT Hub** as ingress
- **Azure Stream Analytics** or **Synapse Data Explorer** for processing
- **Cosmos DB** or **Synapse SQL** for output storage
- Visualize via **Power BI**

Optionally, archive raw data to **Azure Data Lake** and use **Synapse Pipelines** for batch processing.

Monitoring and Troubleshooting

Q: What's the best way to monitor distributed systems in Azure?

A:

- Use **Application Insights** for app telemetry
- Use **Log Analytics** for querying logs across resources
- Enable **Azure Monitor Alerts** for thresholds and failures
- Use **Correlation IDs** for tracing requests across services

Create dashboards to observe request rates, failures, latency, and infrastructure health.

Q: How can I reduce noisy alerts and focus on actionable signals?

A:

- Tune alert thresholds based on historical metrics
- Group alerts using **Action Groups** and **smart groups**
- Use **dynamic thresholds** in Azure Monitor
- Implement **runbooks or auto-healing** with Azure Automation

---

Miscellaneous

Q: How do I manage costs effectively in Azure?

A:

- Use **Azure Cost Management + Budgets**
- Tag resources by team/project/environment
- Use **Reserved Instances** for predictable workloads
- Right-size VMs, databases, and scale limits
- Use **spot instances** for batch and interruptible jobs
- Schedule non-prod resources to shut down automatically

Summary

The journey through Azure architecture and cloud design brings about many common questions—some strategic, others tactical. This FAQ serves as a reference for answering high-frequency queries and reinforcing best practices. Bookmark this section as a go-to guide during design reviews, project planning, and troubleshooting sessions.

Key advice across all questions:

- Favor managed services when possible
- Design for failure and observability
- Automate consistently
- Evolve iteratively—architectures grow with your application

Stay curious, stay updated, and build responsibly in the cloud.

www.ingramcontent.com/pod-product-compliance
Lightning Source LLC
LaVergne TN
LVHW090301210926
848480LV00001B/94
* 9 7 9 8 2 3 1 2 3 9 5 8 0 *